THE
POLTERGEIST
CASEBOOK

JOHN WEST

Published 2025 by arima publishing

www.arimapublishing.co.uk

ISBN 978 1 84549 850 4

© John West 2025

All rights reserved

This book is copyright. Subject to statutory exception and to provisions of relevant collective licensing agreements, no part of this publication may be reproduced, stored in a retrieval system, or transmitted in any form or by any means, without the prior written permission of the author.

This book is sold subject to the conditions that it shall not, by way of trade or otherwise, be lent, re-sold, hired out, or otherwise circulated without the publisher's prior consent in any form of binding or cover other than that which it is published and without a similar condition including this condition being imposed on the subsequent purchaser.

arima publishing

www.arimapublishing.com

Dedicated to the memory of Colin Wilson,
Elliott O'Donnell, Peter Underwood, Harry Price,
Andrew Green, Guy Lyon Playfair, Maurice Grosse and
Sir Arthur Conan Doyle – seekers of the truth.

Front cover design: Jason Figgis.
Images on frontispiece and pages 11, 35, 65, and 76 courtesy of John West.
Image on page 18 courtesy of Stewart Evans.

CONTENTS

Foreword
Whispers from Orwell Park - Jason Figgis 1

Preface
A Life Touched by the Unseen - John West 3

Introduction by Damon Wilson
The Impossible in Everyday Life 5

Chapter One
The Haunted Child: Annie Cleave and the Durweston Mystery 11

Chapter Two
Poltergeists Through the Ages: Echoes of Fear, Faith, and Frenzy 15

Chapter Three
A Harmless Joker? 21

Chapter Four
The Seven Stages of the Poltergeist 25

Chapter Five
The Devil in the Hearth: Poltergeists, Witchcraft, and Fear in the
17th Century 29

Chapter Six
The Drummer of Tedworth 35

Chapter Seven
The Epworth Rectory Haunting 41

Chapter Eight
The Cock Lane Haunting 45

Chapter Nine
The Outsider Investigates: Colin Wilson and the Poltergeist Enigma 51

Chapter Ten
The Split Brain 55

Chapter Eleven
Earth Energies and Place-Centred Poltergeists 61

Chapter Twelve
Poltergeists and Possessed Relics 65

Chapter Thirteen
The Black Monk of Pontefract 73

Chapter Fourteen
The Bell Witch 79

Chapter Fifteen
Interpreting the Unseen: Evidence and Argument in the Age of Spirits 87

Chapter Sixteen
Pete the Poltergeist 91

Chapter Seventeen
Theories, Myths, and Misconceptions 95

Chapter Eighteen
The Enfield Case 101

Chapter Nineteen
The Search for the Truth 111

Afterword
Alan Murdie on the Poltergeist Phenomenon 117

Appendix
The Epworth Rectory Haunting 121

About John West 131

Recommended Reading 133

Other Books by John West 137

Foreword

Whispers from Orwell Park: A Childhood Haunted by Ghosts and Shadows

When I was seven years old in 1974, my family and I moved from the relative bustle of Ranelagh, on the outskirts of Dublin city, to the serenity of a small outer suburban community called Orwell Park, nestled at the foot of the verdant Dublin Mountains.

Our house was the last one on the left in a quiet cul-de-sac, where my father (who was a very literary tanker driver for Irish Industrial Gases) was the only man to own a car — which he required to travel the several cross-city miles to his place of work.

The change of pace was wonderful, and the silence at night — as my brother Peter and I peered into the almost impenetrable gloom to the eerie outline of the ominous ruins of the Hellfire Club, perched like a spectral beacon at the apex of Montpelier Hill on the not-too-distant horizon — was a place of wonder to me.

I, in particular, would settle into my warm blanket at night and read the latest book of true ghost stories, edited by Peter Haining, or fictional tales of the paranormal, edited by Mary Danby and co.

I would get lost in my imagination and wonder, with glee, at what impossible creatures might be crawling through the bushes and small trees of our sizeable back garden, perhaps eyeing the dull glow from our bedroom light and deciding whether to scale the short distance from the mossy path to our window to peer in at our bookish pursuits.

No such creature ever did, but Christmas was a time when we were guaranteed our horrific delights.

When the Radio Times bumper Christmas edition was released, we would scour each page with forensic attention to detail, searching for plays or films that even hinted at the paranormal, and were, of course, always delighted to find that Lawrence Gordon Clark was to treat us yet again to one of his brilliant televisual adaptations of either an M.R. James story (the father of the English short-form ghost story) or the rare and horrific case of Charles Dickens' *The Signalman*.

Christmas was bountiful in this regard. We were never far from ghost stories — either on television, in books, or, in some instances, the spoken word — when our father would recount a chilling tale or two.

But, from 1977 through to around 1979, a large town and district in the northern Greater London area called Enfield loomed large in our imagination.

The Enfield Poltergeist case referred to a series of paranormal events that occurred at a council house in Enfield during those years. The disturbances primarily involved two young sisters, Janet and Margaret Hodgson, aged eleven and thirteen. These events included levitation, objects moving apparently on their own, and, in some instances, the sound of disembodied voices.

Several paranormal investigators, including members of the Society for Psychical Research — most notably Maurice Grosse and Guy Lyon Playfair — analyzed the case, documenting their discoveries through audio recordings, photos, and witness accounts.

Every aspect of this disturbing case seemed tailored to terrify and simultaneously entertain anyone with a lean towards the esoteric and the supernatural.

An interesting synchronicity emerged more than twenty years later when Maurice Grosse wrote me a fabulous letter, praising my Discovery Channel documentary feature *The Twilight Hour*, which followed the work of photographer of the haunted realm, Sir Simon Marsden, as he gathered material for his new book of the same name.

Maurice offered his very considerable services for any future project, but alas, we never got to work together.

What he certainly did inspire, though, was a collaboration with my longtime creative partner, the prolific journalist and bestselling writer (and author of this very volume), John West — not only on this book but also on a soon-to-be-released feature documentary on the subject: *The Poltergeist Casebook* written by John and directed by Yours Truly.

Watch this space!

Jason Figgis, Dublin, 2025

Preface
A Life Touched by the Unseen

I have always been interested in the paranormal. As a child, I often read my mother's paperback books on the subject. I was fascinated by the lurid covers depicting ghostly monks, skeletons, and phantom ladies. Opening the yellowing pages, I would eagerly devour the frightening accounts of headless coachmen, phantom English Civil War soldiers, and Black Shuck, the Hell Hound of East Anglia. My father encouraged my interest in the subject, and he would buy me books by Peter Underwood and Andrew Green, two of the most noted ghost hunters of the 1970s.

Poltergeists have always intrigued me, especially as I grew up in 1970s Enfield, the scene of a famous poltergeist case involving a family living in Green Street. I can remember watching TV news reports and chatting with my friends in the school playground about the weird happenings centred around the teenage girls in the house. I knew Green Street very well, as my mother used to have her hair styled in a salon at the end of the road. On several occasions, I would find myself walking with her along the street and fearfully gazing at what was pointed out as the 'haunted house.' At first, my mother was sceptical about the haunting until she spoke with the lollipop lady, who had witnessed one of the girls levitating by a window.

After that, she was a confirmed believer and would always quicken her pace whenever she had to walk past the house. My father worked for Enfield Council and once had to visit the property with a colleague to unblock the drains. He saw nothing, but his colleague claimed to have seen an object levitating in the garden and fled in terror, leaving my father to finish the job.

My interest in ghosts continued into adult life, and I began writing monthly articles on the subject for *Psychic News* magazine. Books followed, and a meeting with the film director Jason Figgis led me to make films with him, including a series devoted to Colin Wilson, another literary hero of mine. Colin's fascination with the paranormal led him to write numerous books on the subject, one of which focused on poltergeists.

Colin's excellent and informative book inspired me to write a documentary on the subject, and this, in turn, led to this book.

As a child in 1970s Enfield, I could never have imagined that many years later, I would not only be making a documentary on poltergeists but also writing a book devoted to the subject with an introduction by Damon Wilson, the son of my childhood hero, and an afterword by Alan Murdie, chairman of the world-famous Ghost Club. Sometimes, reality certainly surpasses the imagination!

John West, Suffolk, 2025

Introduction

The Impossible in Everyday Life

By Damon Wilson

My father, Colin Wilson, had leapt to international fame in 1956, aged just 25 years old. His first published book – *The Outsider* – was a highly intelligent yet accessible philosophical investigation of the many 'lost geniuses' that our civilisation seems to produce. Over the next decade or so, Dad wrote many other books; not just philosophy but also existentialist novels, science fiction, criminology and detective thrillers.

Then, in the early 1970s, Dad was approached by Random House, a prestigious publisher who wanted to commission a comprehensive study on the subject of the paranormal. Dad, of course, said no – he was a serious investigator, not a kooky hack. But the publisher stressed that was why they wanted him – he was both openminded and cautious of unsubstantiated flights of fantasy.

So my father took the commission, and the resulting book – *The Occult* (Random House, 1971) – was a bestseller. It was also a very long, very thorough investigation of aspects of the paranormal, from the study of ESP to Kabbalistic theories of magic; from the philosophy of George Ivanovich Gurdjieff to the haunting of Borley Rectory. And my father's conclusion? That there is simply too much evidence of occult events to be rejected wholesale as trickery or delusion.

Following the publication of *The Occult*, the mix of visitors changed slightly. There were still many journalists and fellow authors – like the future Poet Laureate, John Betjeman. However, there were now a lot more people that some would call 'weird'. In my childhood, I met self-proclaimed witches, the psychic detective Robert Cracknell (a jolly, down-to-earth man who also ran a debt collection agency) and famous paranormal investigators like Guy Playfair and Stanley Krippner.

One of Dad's visitors deeply affected me personally. A journalist called Joe Fisher was invited down to Cornwall after sending Dad the manuscript of his book *Hungry Ghosts* (later published by Grafton in 1991). I, then in my mid-twenties, was also visiting Mum and Dad and got chatting to Joe. His story was fascinating, and we talked for hours. I remember him as a clever, good-natured man who had clearly undergone a very traumatic experience.

In 1984 Joe Fisher was living in Canada and was working as a freelance journalist. He investigated a local channeller – a woman who, under hypnosis, had started to speak in the voices of 'ghosts'. Joe was, of course, suspicious, but the fact that the channeller made no profit from the sessions (she spoke while being hypnotised to help with pain relief for her cancer) and the many details the apparently dead spirits gave about their lives more than half-convinced him. Then he did deeper research on their stories and found that they were false.

The voice of a 19th century Yorkshire farmer, for example, had given a very precise and accurate description of his local Yorkshire countryside – but the parish records showed that a farmer of that name had never existed. A supposed RAF fighter pilot had given a very accurate description of the history of his squadron – but no one of his name had ever flown with them.

So, case closed, you might think: a simple matter of fraud or delusion. But Joe had spent many hours talking to these entities, and he was sure that there was more to it than that. The 'things' were indeed lying about what they were, but, he believed, they had solid and consistent identities of their own. He concluded that these were real beings, hungry for attention or some other type of psychological or psychic feeding. But they were liars, and Joe called them that in his book.

When I met Joe, he said he felt cursed by the ongoing resentment of the beings he had confronted.

In 2001, Joe stepped off a cliff in Ontario and was killed. In the update of his 1991 book (*The Siren Call of Hungry Ghosts* (Paraview Press, 2001) Joe claimed that he had suffered continuous bad luck since the original publication. It is hard to believe that his death was entirely accidental, especially after his publisher reported that Joe had told them that 'the spirits were still after him for having written his final book.' I personally think that Joe committed suicide, but I also believe that his conviction that he was being hounded by supernatural beings was a clear factor in his decision to end his life.

Now you are going on to read John's book. You will find it full of people like Joe Fisher – bemused and frightened witnesses to apparently impossible physical events. And those events are driven by something that looks like impish or sometimes malevolent intelligence. Thus the poltergeist lies at the heart of so many paranormal mysteries.

Physical objects cannot be moved, except when there is a direct physical force acting on them; this is basic Newtonian physics. Yet thousands of witnesses over the centuries have reported poltergeists moving and even instantly transporting solid objects. This is either impossible – in which case we have to believe that *all* the witnesses are either liars or deluded – or we should accept that forces are acting that we do not understand.

In June 1752, Ben Franklin - the Philadelphia publisher, politician and natural philosopher - flew a kite during a storm. Attached to the kite were a metal key and a Leyden jar (a type of experimental electrical storage battery). The kite was not struck by lightning – or Franklin would probably have been electrocuted. But the key collected enough ambient electrical energy to charge the battery.

What Franklin was doing – with his usual sense of dramatic style – was illustrating a line of scientific research that was still in its infancy. To most people in 1752, lightning was a mystery best explained by preachers, not natural philosophers.

What Franklin so brilliantly illustrated was the fact that lightning – and electricity in general – could potentially be harnessed for the use of human beings: an astounding demonstration for the mid-eighteenth century, but now so commonplace an idea that we take it for granted (until there is a power cut).

Electromagnetic energy is invisible in most circumstances, but it powers our civilisation. Yet in the many millennia before the eighteenth century, anyone who suggested 'harnessing the lightning' would have been seen as a fantasist or a lunatic.

Lightning was a natural phenomenon that everyone had seen at one time or another, but our ancestors just didn't have the tools to better utilise that knowledge. So, whatever energy that poltergeists might be using may one day be better understood and used by people.

Apparent poltergeist intelligence is a harder nut to crack. Memory is a defining factor of human intelligence; it is the toolkit that we dive into whenever we have to solve a problem. And memory, as we understand it, absolutely requires a physical brain to hold the recording of our life experiences. Thus, people who suffer brain damage often lose part or all of their memory – usually permanently. The brain is an intricate structure of neural pathways that we build and restructure through our ongoing life experiences.

For example, I have largely overcome that dyslexia that plagued my school days. Working very long hours as a writer on a computer gaming magazine, over several years, I inadvertently rewired my neural network to overcome my dyslexic problem with spelling. Unless I think directly about how to spell a word, that is… then I become self-conscious, my brain almost audibly clicks back into my old, dyslexic pathways and I can't spell again until I make myself relax. In both cases I am using separate sets of recorded experiences (i.e., memories) to deal with a spelling problem.

So how can a poltergeist – with no apparent brain structure – manage to write readable messages on walls and even talk understandable phrases from the empty air?

Likewise, our emotions rely on certain glands – like the adrenal gland – that are essential to providing the physical effect of emotional reaction. Yet poltergeists seem to be very emotional beings, without this apparently essential equipment.

But to take such a mechanistic view of human existence – that we are meat machines who simply think that we think – is also rather unscientific. It is based on the idea that what we know of human intelligence is all there is to know - that there are no hidden mechanisms to our consciousness that are beyond our present understanding.

It seems to me – and here I am wading deep into the waters of pure speculation – that there is a possible mechanism that may explain this seeming scientific standoff. It starts from the fact that there are indeed living human brains involved in *all* poltergeist cases: those of the witnesses.

As John will so carefully illustrate, there are two main strands of explanation for the existence of poltergeists. One is that they are the result of unconscious telekinetic actions created by nearby people – a sort of multiple personality disorder married to an as-yet-unmapped power of mind over matter. The other – that my father eventually favoured – was that poltergeists are what they usually claim to be – disembodied spirits, maybe of the dead.

So how could a human mind survive death when the all-important brain is rotting to mush in the corpse's skull? The respected psychiatrist Carl Jung suggested that all human minds might be telepathically connected on the subconscious level – what he called the 'collective unconscious'. Jung described this phenomenon as a 'psychic system of a collective, universal, and impersonal nature which is identical in all individuals'. Jung thought the collective unconscious was a sort of pooled library of archetypal beliefs and shared instincts, only accessible by our subconscious minds.

If this theory is true, then it is not too big a jump to believe that human memories, even of long-dead ancestors, might also survive in the collective unconscious of the living human population. Science recognises that our brains record almost everything that happens to us in startling detail, but that it is the recall ability of our conscious minds that is so flawed. As Jung suggested, maybe much else is stored in our brains, beyond the access of our waking minds.

So perhaps the subconscious part of a human mind, under certain stressful circumstances, can re-activate the memory structure of a dead mind: in effect, mentally reanimate a dead person. As noted above, human intelligence might simplistically be described as living consciousness acting through the filter of past memories, trained instincts and ingrained reactions. But do those memories, instincts and reactions *have* to originate in the body of the human in question? The controversial psychological concept of dissociative identity disorder (previously known as multiple personality syndrome) suggests that the human subconscious mind can create and run several distinct 'people' from the same body. Is this what is happening in a poltergeist incident?

Here I'm asking the reader to consider several (as-yet) unproven paranormal theories: the collective unconscious; ancestral or genetic memory; telepathy; telekinesis; dissociative identity disorder and/or possession by the memory structures of dead people. Taken together, we have the mechanics of a process that might, in the right circumstances, produce the poltergeist 'hauntings' described in this book. It is a scientific truism that one can't explain one unproved phenomenon by citing another unproved phenomenon (let alone five or six). But that was also true of Ben Franklin trying to show that the channelling and storage of lightning was a possibility…

Read John's excellent book, and you will be in a good position to come to your own conclusions. After all, consideration and evaluation of the available evidence is the first step towards any world-shaking scientific discovery.

Damon Wilson, Norfolk, 2025

Chapter One

The Haunted Child: Annie Cleave and the Durweston Mystery

"The annoyances appear rather like the tricks of a mischievous imp. I refer to what the Germans call the Poltergeist, or racketing spectre, for all the phenomenon is known in all countries and has been known in all ages."
— *Catherine Crowe, The Night Side of Nature*, 1848. Her book of supernatural stories introduced the word 'poltergeist' into the English language.

The phenomenon we now call the *poltergeist* has long existed at the uneasy intersection of folklore, fear, and fact—where noisy spirits, mischievous and malevolent, disturb the peace of ordinary homes. Though often dismissed as superstition or hysteria, such stories persist, passed down through generations and backed, in some cases, by compelling testimony. One of the most curious and poignant of these accounts emerged from the quiet village of Durweston, Dorset, in the winter of 1894–95. The Durweston case offers an early and striking example of the classic poltergeist narrative—and a troubling glimpse into the strange bond between trauma, adolescence, and the unexplained.

The mystery began in the quiet home of Mrs. Best, a woman in her sixties, who had opened her door—and her heart—to two orphaned sisters from the workhouse. Thirteen-year-old Annie Cleave and her four-year-old sister, Gertie, had been given a chance at a new life. But what followed was anything but ordinary. The strange events that would soon grip the small Dorset village of Durweston were first reported in the *Western Gazette* on January 11, 1895.

"The little village of Durweston, three miles from Blandford, has been for some weeks past the scene of considerable excitement in consequence of the supposition that one of the cottages is haunted.

The cottage in question is at Norton, a spot isolated from the rest of the village, some considerable distance from the highway, and on the outskirts of a wood. The cottages are owned by Viscount Portman; his keeper (named Newman) occupies one, and the other, until recently, has been in the occupation of a widow (named Mrs. Best) and two little orphan girls, who were boarded out to Mrs. Best by the Hon. Misses Pitt of Stepleton. It is in the latter house that these occurrences took place, which have caused such a scare in the village. It is more than a month since Mrs. Best—who, it may be stated here, is a most respectable woman of a quiet, inoffensive disposition and on good terms with her neighbours and the village generally—became puzzled by faint knocking and scratching in various parts of the house and could account for the same in no possible way..."

Mr. Newman could even hear the knocking sounds next door. Reports also quoted the village blacksmith as describing the noises as "as heavy as sledgehammer blows."

The Society for Psychical Research was informed of the case and sent one of its members, Mr. Westlake, to investigate. He interviewed 20 witnesses and discovered that the disturbances had started on December 13, 1894. Mr. Newman told him that he was called next door on December 18 and informed that Annie had seen a boot suddenly appear in the garden and strike the back door, leaving a muddy mark. Newman also reported that, as he sat in Mrs. Best's cottage, beads and a toy whistle struck the window. Amusingly, he shouted back, "You're a coward, you're a coward; why don't you throw money?"

However, he was to be disappointed. The door creaked open, and—one by one— several small shells began to float silently into the room. They moved at intervals of roughly half a minute, gliding through the air with uncanny slowness, as if suspended in an invisible current. Each object drifted with such delicate grace that, when they touched him, the sensation was barely noticeable—like the brush of a cobweb.

Then came two thimbles, hovering forward with the same strange control. They moved so gradually, so impossibly gently, that under normal circumstances they would have fallen to the floor long before reaching him. And yet, they arrived—unhindered and deliberate.

Throughout this bizarre display, the two children remained quietly seated in the room, never leaving his sight.

It is worth emphasizing just how rare this kind of phenomenon is. In most poltergeist cases, objects are found displaced or are flung violently across rooms—sudden, chaotic events. But here, the movement was almost elegant, unnervingly slow, as though guided by an unseen intelligence. Few such cases include the direct witnessing of objects in controlled, deliberate flight—making this encounter all the more extraordinary.

Then, from directly below his seat, a slate pencil appeared, followed by a hasp—similar to the one on his glove—which dropped onto his lap from a point above head level. A boot then entered the room from outside the door, moving about a foot above the ground before pitching down beside him. The same boot had previously fallen in front of the door. Mrs. Best had thrown it out, but now it had returned. After that, Newman went outside, placed his foot firmly on the boot, and declared, "I defy anything to move this boot." No sooner had he stepped away than the boot rose up behind him and knocked his hat off. The boot and the hat fell to the ground together.

Small stones would also fly through the windows, breaking the glass. Annie claimed to have seen "a queer animal with a green head and green eyes and a big bushy tail, sitting up and pulling her doll to pieces with its paws." Annie called her sister, who saw it too.

A few days later, the girls and Mrs. Best moved into Newman's cottage. On January 10, the Reverend. W. M. Anderson and the local schoolmaster, Mr. Sheppard, visited the home. Mrs. Best took the girls to bed, deciding to stay with them. The room was filled with loud rapping sounds and scratches on the walls. Anderson placed his ear and head against the wall but could detect no vibrations. However, when he rested his head on the rail at the bottom of the bed, he distinctly felt vibrations that varied with the loudness of the knocking. From time to time, a noise could be heard within the wall, as though someone were scratching it with their nails. When the rapping first began, he observed that it often stopped when he entered the room. But after a short while, his presence no longer seemed to matter— the noise continued, loud and unrelenting.

Mr. Sheppard asked the entity to communicate through raps. Using a specified number of knocks for "yes," it was asked to write on a slate. When asked where the slate should be placed, the entity requested it be put on a windowsill. At 2:30 a.m., the entity asked that only the two girls and Mrs. Best remain in the room. The rest of the group was to wait downstairs, taking the light with them.

At first, only scratches appeared on the slate. Anderson and Sheppard asked it to try again. This time, it drew curves they described as "beautifully drawn," with firm, bold lines "such as no child could produce." The words MONY and GARDEN then appeared on the slate. However, a later search of the garden found nothing.

Amid perfect silence, everyone in the room clearly heard the sound of a pencil scratching across the slate, Reverend Anderson later recalled. He noted that any movement by anyone in the bed would have been immediately obvious to him, and he was absolutely certain that the writing could not have been done by anyone present without his noticing. He told Mrs. Best that he was personally convinced no one had moved, let alone left the bed—which was positioned at least four feet from the window. In response, Mrs. Best stated that she was willing to take a solemn oath that neither she nor the girls had moved or left the bed during the incident.

Annie and Gertie were sent to stay with the Cross family in Durweston. The noises followed them. Their room was filled with rapping and scratching sounds, even as the girls slept soundly. Plaster fell from the walls, and the poltergeist was heard tapping out a tune. Mr. Cross requested "comic, school, and sacred songs," and all were answered by raps on the headboard, matching each single note. "The only tune we asked for which was not rapped out was *The British Grenadiers*," Cross later said.

The two girls were separated. Annie was taken to a lady's house in Iwerne Minster. Unexplained noises were reported there too, and a large stone was thrown onto the porch roof. Snowdrops were also found scattered around the garden. On March 7, Miss M. H. Mason, a board inspector for foster children, visited and decided to relocate Annie to a flat in London. No further strange activity was reported, and a doctor who examined the girl declared her to be hysterical, with a consumptive tendency. Annie is believed to have died of tuberculosis a few years later. It is not known what became of her sister, Gertie.

The Durweston case may not be well-known today, but it remains a striking example of a classic poltergeist haunting. From inexplicable knocks and flying objects to mysterious writing on a slate, the events described in this quiet Dorset village have all the hallmarks that continue to fascinate and baffle us.

What makes this case especially compelling is the credibility of those involved— clergy, schoolteachers, and ordinary villagers—none of whom had anything to gain by fabricating such claims. Instead, they reported what they saw and heard, even when it defied explanation.

The story of Annie Cleave and the paranormal forces that seemed to follow her offers a haunting reminder that not all mysteries fade quietly into the past.

Chapter Two
Poltergeists Through the Ages: Echoes of Fear, Faith, and Frenzy

So what are poltergeists—the German word for 'noisy spirit' or 'rumbling ghost'? Are they ghosts? Are they demons? Or do they stem from the psychic energy of an emotionally disturbed adolescent expressing itself in ways beyond our current comprehension?

Whatever they may be, poltergeists are certainly not a modern phenomenon. Accounts of hauntings—now recognised as classic poltergeist behaviour—are found throughout history. For example, the Roman historian Suetonius, in his book *Lives of the Caesars*, writes of the villa where Augustus, Rome's first emperor, was supposedly born:

"A small room like a pantry is shown to this day as the emperor's nursery in his grandfather's country house near Velitrae, and the opinion prevails in the neighbourhood that he was actually born there. No one ventures to enter this room except of necessity and after purification, since there is a conviction of long-standing that those who approach it without ceremony are seized with shuddering and terror; and what is more, this has recently been shown to be true. For when a new owner, either by chance or to test the matter, went to bed in that room, it came to pass that, after a very few hours of the night, he was thrown out by a sudden mysterious force and was found—bedclothes and all—half-dead before the door."

The *Annales Fuldenses*, a chronicle dating back to 858 AD, records another early case. An 'evil spirit' plagued a farmhouse near Bingen in Germany, throwing stones and hammering on the walls. The farmer was the apparent object of the spirit's hatred, for it followed him around and burnt his crops soon after they were gathered. The entity also spoke, denouncing the man for committing adultery. One version of the story, as recorded in a medieval book called *The Golden Legend*, also claims that priests sent to bless the house had stones thrown at them. It added that the spirit was the 'familiar' of a priest who had committed adultery.

In the twelfth century, the medieval historian and priest Gerald of Wales, while travelling through his native land, came to hear of two haunted houses in Pembrokeshire. Unclean spirits were believed to be in close communication with human beings. Though invisible, their presence was unmistakably felt. These entities reportedly manifested first in the home of a man named Stephen Wiriet and later in the residence of William Nott. In both cases, the spirits made their presence known by throwing filth and other objects around the house. Their behaviour appeared more mischievous than malevolent, as if they were playing games rather than intending harm.

In William Nott's house, the spirit was particularly destructive to household items. It targeted both linen and woollen garments belonging to the host and his guests, tearing them and punching holes through the fabric. No precautions proved effective in preventing this damage—neither the care taken by the residents nor physical barriers within the home offered any protection.

Stephen Wiriet's house, however, was the scene of an even greater marvel. The spirit there reportedly engaged in direct conversation with the inhabitants. When people mocked or insulted it—as they often did for amusement—the entity would respond by publicly recounting shameful or secret events from their past, things they would have preferred to remain hidden.

Gerald also writes that sprinkling the places with holy water and saying prayers made no difference. It made things worse, as the priests had filth thrown at them upon entering the houses. Seeking a reason for the hauntings, Gerald proposed that the abrupt shift from wealth to poverty could have played a role, given that both men later faced financial difficulties, with the poltergeist warning them that their circumstances were about to change.

Three hundred years later, in 1599, Martin del Rio wrote of spectres known to appear at certain times and in particular homes, where they caused a variety of disturbances and annoyances. Some of these entities disrupted sleep by clattering pots or hurling stones across rooms, while others were reported to go so far as to drag away mattresses and toss sleepers out of their beds.

Over the centuries, people have blamed the Devil, demons, witchcraft, fairies, or tormented souls for these outbreaks of poltergeist activity. Gerald believed that demons were to blame, while Tertullian, an early Christian author from the Roman province of Carthage, firmly believed that the phenomenon was caused by unhappy ghosts: "It seems credible that these souls in particular, whom a cruel and untimely death has violently and unfairly wrenched from life, should contribute to violence and injustice, as if in retaliation for their hurt."

The Rev. Robert Kirk, the 17th-century author of *The Secret Commonwealth of Elves, Fauns & Fairies*, did not agree and attributed the phenomenon to fairies: "The invisible Wights which haunt Houses... throw great Stones, Pieces of Earth and Wood, at the inhabitants, [but] they hurt them not at all."

However, he also wrote that others believed restless spirits were involved: "Those creatures that move invisibly in a house, and cast great stones, but do not do much hurt" were "souls that have not attained their rest."

Whatever was behind the phenomenon, one thing was becoming increasingly clear: one person was usually the focal point of these hauntings—an individual emotionally troubled or disturbed in some way.

Christina of Stommeln, who the Catholic Church later declared a saint, is a case in point. Growing up in the 13th century, she began to experience religious visions from the age of five. At ten, she had a dream in which Christ told her she would live with a religious order—the Beguines. When she reached twelve, her parents arranged her marriage, but she left without their permission and joined a Beguine community in Cologne. Determined to dedicate her life to Christ, she began to exhibit behaviours that even her contemporaries thought might indicate she was insane. She was convinced the consecrated host contained maggots or would turn into a toad if she swallowed it. Forced to leave the community, she returned home and was taken in by a parish priest, Johannes.

Now in her twenties, with her religious mania increasing, Christina told the priest that the Devil would appear and beat her, lifting her bedclothes and gnawing at her flesh "like a dog." To a modern observer, it would be easy to dismiss her claims as unbalanced religious fanaticism—but there were other witnesses.

Once, Christina and several others were praying in church when a filthy bag flew down the length of the nave and landed at their feet. Inside was Christina's prayer book, which she claimed had been stolen by the Devil three months earlier. Others also witnessed attacks. Peter of Dacia, a Dominican friar who befriended her, saw Christina and her visitors pelted with faeces. When a priest attempted an exorcism, a loud bang was heard, the candle went out, and the exorcist was covered in human waste.

Over time, the attacks worsened. Stones and bones were thrown about, clothes and shoes were ripped or destroyed, priests were attacked and bitten, and the severed head of a cat was thrust into Christina's mouth. Once, she was pulled out of bed by her hair. Her sister, rushing to help, was stabbed in the back by a sword waving in mid-air. A priest entering the room was also attacked. A skull materialised, uttering words, while stones and nails appeared embedded in Christina's flesh. Falling into trances, she would exhibit stigmatic signs on her feet, head, and hands. However, with the death of Peter of Dacia in 1288, Christina's mystical experiences ceased.

This shocking case bears many striking similarities to that of the Romanian girl Eleonore Zugun, who in 1925 became the focus of a poltergeist attack involving being bitten and thrown out of bed. Stigmatic signs also appeared on her face and arms.

Eleonore's troubles began after an argument with her grandmother—a woman reputed to be a witch—following an incident in February 1925, when she was eleven. While visiting her grandmother, she found a coin in the road. Ignoring warnings that it was "the Devil's money," she used it to buy sweets, refusing to share them. Her grandmother angrily told her that she had "swallowed the Devil" and would never be free of him.

Eleonore was sent to a monastery for an exorcism and later confined to a mental asylum as the activity continued. A local newspaper mentioned the case, attracting the attention of a German spiritualist organisation. Fritz Grunewald, an eminent German engineer and parapsychologist, investigated and managed to remove her from the asylum and return her to the monastery, where he observed her for the next few days. He later published a statement in which he stated the poltergeist activity was genuine.

Harry Price.

At thirteen, Eleonore came under the protection of Countess Zoe Wassilko-Serecki, an Austrian parapsychologist and psychoanalyst. She took Eleonore to live with her in Vienna, where she witnessed repeated poltergeist attacks—claiming to have experienced over 1,000 incidents in three months. Harry Price, the noted paranormal researcher and author, also observed Eleonore in Vienna and at his London laboratory, documenting the case in *Poltergeist Over England*.

Observed phenomena included:

Rapping sounds. Harry Price described them as "similar to those heard so often with many mediums. No attempt has been made to extract information from, or to communicate with, any entity or personality assumed to be responsible for the phenomena; in fact, it is not thought possible to do so by this means, as the raps are purely spontaneous and cannot be induced by the methods usually employed."

Object displacement. These included three valuable chess pieces from a set owned by the countess's father; they reappeared after three days, seemingly falling from the air. On another occasion, pieces of cloth meant to serve as a bodice for Eleonore vanished from a table. The cloth was never found.

Bite marks, abrasions, and weals on Eleonore's skin. Price wrote of observing Eleonore crying out in pain and pointing to a part of her body. She would reveal a red bite mark upon lifting her clothing. The examination revealed that some of these marks were wet. The 'saliva' contained microorganisms that differed from those in Eleonore's saliva.

Automatic writing. Wassilko asked Eleonore to try automatic writing, resulting in communications from 'Dracu.' These messages would promise to produce phenomena on a certain day. Sometimes the phenomenon would occur as promised, but on other occasions, it would not.

A disembodied voice. Learning that a friend of Eleonore was seriously ill, the girl fretted over it and expressed hope to the countess that her friend would get better. Suddenly a 'lifeless' and hollow-sounding voice answered from behind them, near the ceiling, promising her friend would recover.

On 14 February 1927, Eleonore experienced her first menstrual period. The phenomena then declined dramatically, with the final occurrences recorded on 17 June.

The Countess concluded the poltergeist activity was an unconscious expression of Eleonore's mind, possibly linked to suppressed sexual urges toward her father. She thought the attacks, especially the scratches and bite marks, were a form of self-punishment.

The Zugun case proved highly influential in promoting the idea that poltergeists were sexual in origin, applying Freudian psychoanalysis to an active poltergeist haunting. Wassilko-Serecki further proposed a link between the distribution of phenomena and the girl's menstrual cycle development. Baron von Schrenck-Notzing, a German physician, psychiatrist, and psychical researcher, supported the Countess's research with a substantial grant; however, Schrenck-Notzing proposed that the events followed the lunar cycle (the idea that the menstrual and lunar cycles are interconnected is widespread). However, it

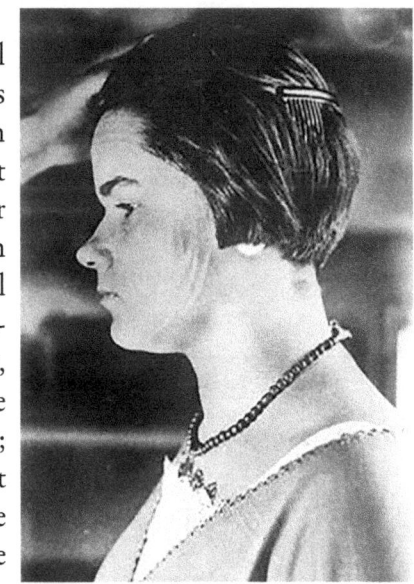

Scratch marks on Eleonore Zugun's face.

should be noted that a recent analysis of the data by Professor Peter Mulacz, a member of the Parapsychological Association, indicates that the phenomenon was not linked to any peaks in the girl's menstrual cycle. The idea that Eleonore's repressed sexual urges for her father were the catalyst for the poltergeist outbreak has also been called into question by researchers and students of the case.

As this chapter illustrates, long before the word *poltergeist* entered the English language, stories of violent, unseen forces shaking homes, hurling objects, and tormenting individuals were already embedded in our history. From ancient Roman accounts and medieval chronicles to the disturbing tales of Christina of Stommeln and Eleonore Zugun, these phenomena have followed strikingly similar patterns across cultures and centuries.

What emerges from these cases is a portrait of the poltergeist not merely as a "noisy ghost," but as a phenomenon that seems to erupt in moments of emotional, psychological, or spiritual unrest—often centered on young women navigating trauma, religious fervor, or the upheaval of adolescence.

Chapter Three

A Harmless Joker?

Even today, popular myth frequently portrays the poltergeist as a harmless prankster—an entity incapable of causing significant harm to its human victims. However, as we have seen, they can have a darker side, often acting like spoilt children who can quickly turn to violence after initial displays of friendship and goodwill. Maria Jose Ferreira, a girl in Brazil, is just another example of how a friendly poltergeist can suddenly change into something far less pleasant.

The haunting began in December 1965, with falling bricks suddenly appearing in the girl's home. The Catholic family called in a priest, who performed an exorcism, but this only made things worse. Stones and eggs would be thrown about whenever Maria was in the home; one stone was found to weigh over eight pounds. On one occasion, several eggs vanished from a refrigerator, reappearing under a chicken in the backyard. The family sought advice from a neighbour, João Volpe, who was a spiritualist. Volpe said that Maria was a natural medium who unwittingly allowed the poltergeist phenomena to occur.

The stone-throwing continued, with stones now appearing from the ceiling. One fell apart, the pieces seeming to retain some magnetic attraction when reassembled. A second stone materialised, tapping three individuals on the head before hitting the floor. The people reported experiencing the sensation of a "ball of compressed air" striking them.

Treating the poltergeist almost like a playmate, Maria would ask for sweets or gifts, such as a brooch. These would suddenly appear at her feet. However, this playful behaviour was short-lived. The girl suddenly faced slaps and bites and had chairs, a large sofa, and even a gas cylinder thrown at her. The attacks continued even when Maria was asleep. The poltergeist pulled pictures and a mirror off the walls and flung them across the room. It smashed crockery and placed cups and glasses over her mouth, seemingly attempting to suffocate her. Needles appeared in her skin; on one occasion, fifty-five needles were removed from her heel. The poltergeist always tore off the bandages covering her wounds.

On March 14, 1966, Maria's clothing was seen smouldering as she was eating her lunch at school. That same day, the Volpes' bedroom burst into flames, with Mr. Volpe being badly burnt after grabbing a pillow that appeared to be burning from the inside. Maria was taken to Chico Xavier, Brazil's best-known medium, who claimed that Maria had been a witch in a previous life and was now being persecuted by her victims. The medium treated Maria with prayers and spiritual healing, leading to a decrease in the phenomenon. Now 13 years old, Maria returned to her mother but tragically took her own life in 1970 after consuming a pesticide-laced soft drink.

Another example of poltergeists' unpredictable and violent behaviour is recorded by Nicholas Remy, a French historian and advocate in the 1500s, who wrote of a peasant's cottage in the village of Colombiers. A 'demon' invaded the home, hurling stones at the inhabitants without causing them any harm. Soon, the peasants grew accustomed to this and began to ridicule the entity. The being retaliated by burning the cottage to the ground.

In November 1761, a poltergeist appeared at the Lamb Inn in Bristol, tenanted by Richard Giles and his family. Initially, it disturbed the two young children, Molly (13) and Dobby (8), by rapping and scratching near or within their bedroom. However, the activity quickly escalated, with the children suffering bites, pinches, and cuts from an invisible assailant. Mr. Henry Durbin, a local druggist, investigated the case. He wrote of having witnessed an attack on one of the girls: "I saw Dobby wiping her hands in a towel. While I was talking to her, she cried out [and] was bitten in the neck. I looked and saw the mark of teeth—about eighteen—and wet with spittle."

Mr. Durbin and several others also witnessed one of the girls being strangled by an invisible entity. "I saw the flesh at the side of her throat pushed in, whitish, as if done with fingers, though I saw none."

The poltergeist, now communicating through a series of coded knocking, identified itself as having been summoned by a witch from Mangotsfield, hired by a rival of Richard Giles. Durbin continued his investigation, bringing in several ministers of the church who questioned the spirit in Hebrew, Latin, and Greek.

The haunting continued. The two girls were thrown from their beds so violently that three men were unable to hold them down. The family separated the girls and sent them to stay with friends. With this action, the poltergeist calmed down.

Richard Giles died in May 1762 while returning from Bath, after his horse saddle broke. The poltergeist claimed that witchcraft had killed him. The children returned home, and the phenomenon started up again. Still communicating with Durbin, the poltergeist said the witch had received additional money to prolong the family's suffering. It was decided to bring in a 'cunning woman,' who claimed to have used her powers of white magic to banish the poltergeist forever. The haunting had lasted over a year.

Fortunately, not all poltergeists are as hostile. Some take delight in trying to scare their victims by using less violent means. Martin Luther, the German theologian and religious reformer who initiated the Protestant Reformation in the 16th century, had a personal encounter with a poltergeist in 1521 when staying in Wartburg Castle. A bag of hazelnuts in his possession was seen to jump around his room; at one point, the bag jumped so high that it hit the ceiling. His bed shook, and the sound of invisible barrels rolling about his room further disturbed him. Interestingly, after Luther had left the castle, a lady took up residence in the same room and experienced the same thing. So, was the room, rather than the person, the focus of this particular poltergeist?

Luther had an amusing suggestion about how one should deal with poltergeists— something that he believed to be the work of the Devil. Seventeen years after his experience at the castle, he was told by a minister of a church in Stupitz that for the past year, Satan had been throwing crockery about his home and generally making a nuisance of himself. The minister even heard the Devil laughing as flying pots just missed his head. Things had gotten so bad that the man, his wife, and their children wanted to move. Luther told them to stand firm and command Satan to leave the house. He also added that a lady from Magdeburg, also troubled by similar activity, had driven the Devil away by farting in his presence. However, Luther cautioned, "This example is not always to be followed and is dangerous."

Despite its reputation as a trickster, the poltergeist is no laughing matter. As this chapter has shown, what may begin with misplaced objects or playful tapping can quickly spiral into something far more sinister—biting, scratching, burning, even attempted suffocation. Whether interpreted as the wrath of demons, the mischief of disembodied minds, or the psychic projections of distressed individuals, poltergeist activity seems to follow a familiar arc: attention-seeking chaos that escalates into open hostility.

The case of Maria Jose Ferreira starkly illustrates this progression, moving from small marvels to relentless violence. Others, like the haunting at the Lamb Inn or the fire-starting spirit of Colombiers, only reinforce the idea that these forces— whatever their true nature—are volatile, unpredictable, and deeply personal.

So, is the poltergeist merely a "harmless joker"? The evidence suggests otherwise. It might greet you with a playful knock, but history urges caution before you laugh in return.

Chapter Four
The Seven Stages of the Poltergeist

Although the cause of the poltergeist phenomenon remains the subject of intense debate, researchers in the 20th century began to identify consistent patterns in reported cases. Through careful documentation and analysis, many came to recognize that a typical poltergeist haunting often unfolds in several distinct stages, progressing from minor disturbances to more dramatic and sometimes violent events.

The First Stage: Subtle Disturbances
The haunting begins subtly. Low-level noises—soft scratching, rustling, or tapping—are typically the first signs. These sounds often seem to come from within the walls, ceilings, or beneath the floorboards. Most witnesses dismiss them as the natural creaks of an old house or the movements of rats or mice. In some cases, pets or children are blamed, and no further thought is given to the disturbance—at first.

The Second Stage: Audible Intrusions
As time passes, the noises increase in intensity and variety. What once sounded like faint scratching now becomes raps, bangs, thumps, and heavy footsteps that echo through hallways and staircases. These sounds can come from any direction—walls, ceilings, under furniture—and sometimes seem to follow individuals from room to room.

Witnesses describe rhythmic knocking patterns, sudden crashes, or vibrations in nearby objects. In rare instances, the sound mimics that of a distant explosion, leaving windows rattling. The origin of the noise remains elusive, as no source is ever found.

The Third Stage: Physical Disturbance
At this point, the haunting shifts from sound to movement. Objects within the home begin to move of their own accord. These displacements often occur when no one is watching: a spoon is found in a drawer it was never placed in, a chair turned away from the table. Occasionally, these objects are hot to the touch.

A notable case from Canvey Island in 1709 described a roof tile that slid across the floor "very leisurely and yet so straight, as though it had moved on a line." When a maid retrieved it, the tile was so hot it scorched her palm.

Stones may be thrown with force or fall gently from mid-air, seemingly appearing from nowhere. This phenomenon—so common in such hauntings—is known as *lithobolia*, or "stone-throwing devilry." Some objects shatter on impact, while others land without making a sound.

The Fourth Stage: Apports and Disapports

Unusual phenomena escalate with the appearance—or disappearance—of objects. Small items, such as coins, buttons, or trinkets, may manifest seemingly out of thin air, often falling gently to the ground. These are known as *apports*. In contrast, personal items may vanish without explanation, never to be found again. These are called *disapports*.

Furniture may be rearranged, damaged, or destroyed. Fragile ornaments are found smashed, heirlooms lost. In some cases, prized possessions are reduced to splinters overnight. The intrusion becomes more personal and more difficult to ignore.

The Fifth Stage: Attempts at Communication

Once the entity's presence is firmly established, attempts to communicate often begin. Initially, it responds through coded knocks or raps—one for "yes," two for "no," for example. Over time, these sounds grow more complex, with sequences that suggest intention and even emotion.

Eventually, rudimentary vocalizations emerge: growls, slurps, whistles, or guttural moans. Authors John and Anne Spencer note that "poltergeists do not seem to come with well-developed voices but have to nurture them, usually from small noises and whistles."

These voices, often robotic or mechanical at first, may evolve into more articulate speech. The entity might swear, hurl accusations, or claim to be a variety of unsettling identities: a demon, a witch, the Devil, or the restless spirit of someone who died tragically. Strikingly, these identities often mirror the cultural or religious expectations of the witnesses, as though the poltergeist draws from the household's collective fears.

The Sixth Stage: Escalation and Harm

Suddenly, the activity reaches a terrifying climax. Fires may ignite spontaneously—brief but inexplicable flames that leave little damage yet provoke deep fear. These are rarely destructive but deeply symbolic: a manifestation of chaos, or a warning.

Physical attacks may occur. Victims report scratches that appear while they sleep, bruises with no clear cause, or the sensation of being pinched or shoved.

The poltergeist may claim it will depart soon, and in some cases, even gives a precise date and time. This announcement can mark the beginning of its withdrawal—or signal a final, violent flourish.

The Seventh Stage: Dissolution

Just as suddenly as it began, the haunting ends. The voices grow fainter, the knocking stops, and objects stay still. Sometimes the entity departs overnight, without fanfare. Other times, it recedes slowly, fading over days or even weeks.

No clear reason is given for its departure. Some families report a feeling of peace returning to the house; others are left with lingering anxiety, unsure if the silence will last. Though the phenomena cease, the experience often leaves a lasting psychological imprint on those who endured it.

While sceptics often attribute poltergeist activity to hoaxes, psychological disturbances, or natural causes, the recurrence of distinct stages across cases suggests a phenomenon that is consistent and curiously structured. From faint scratching sounds to violent object displacement and intelligent communication, these stages provide a framework for understanding the seemingly chaotic nature of poltergeist hauntings. As we move forward, the question remains: are poltergeists external spirits, manifestations of inner turmoil, or something else entirely? The seven stages offer clues—but not yet answers.

Chapter Five

The Devil in the Hearth: Poltergeists, Witchcraft, and Fear in the 17th Century

In 17th-century Britain, fear was a constant presence—not just in the form of war or disease, but in the terrifying possibility that unseen forces might invade the household. Poltergeists, witches, and the Devil himself seemed to slip between the cracks of reason and religion, often leaving no trace beyond shattered dishes and broken lives. The lines between psychological disturbance and supernatural torment were not clearly drawn—and, at the time, few dared to question the difference.

During the English Civil War, Paul Fox, a silk weaver from Plaistow in West Ham, was shocked to witness a sword begin flying about a room in the house where he was living. Fox grabbed the sword and took it to another room, placing it on a bench and then locking the door. Despite this, the sword reappeared. A walking stick was also seen hopping up the stairs from the kitchen and dancing around a table, while tiles, pieces of bread, brickbats, and oyster shells flew about the room and broke the windows. In the yard, a stone weighing over half a hundredweight rose and tumbled up the stairs. One brave person who had entered the house to look for signs of trickery was chased out by a "clatter of chairs and stools, candlesticks, and bedstaves." A pipe was also seen to rise from a table and fly across the room. It shattered into several pieces as it hit a wall.

The blame fell on witchcraft. A local woman was accused and held captive in the house, but she was released by a local magistrate, who said she was of good character. It is remarkable that he intervened and freed her—a sign that not all authorities supported the witch craze, even at the height of the witch-hunting frenzy. Despite this, people still wondered whether she had used her powers to cause mischief in the Fox home.

The English Civil War was a time of enormous hardship and fear. Rival armies fighting for political supremacy ravaged the country, causing law and order to collapse. Opportunists like the notorious Matthew Hopkins, the self-appointed Witchfinder General, quickly took advantage of this in East Anglia, using a renewed fear of witchcraft and magic to send many innocents to the gallows on trumped-up charges of sorcery. It was indeed fortunate that the unnamed woman in West Ham was released, for in those troubled times, she could easily have been executed as a witch.

In 1649, following the defeat of the Royalists and the execution of Charles I, Britain became a republic. In 1653, Oliver Cromwell, commander of the army and one of the republic's leading politicians, became Lord Protector following Parliament's failure to govern justly and prepare for new elections. Never the bigot of popular imagination, Cromwell's rule saw a shift towards legal reforms and a more centralized judicial system, which contributed to the decline in withcraft trials.

However, many of his subjects remained convinced of the existence of witchcraft, and a little-known poltergeist case in 1654 only intensified the debate when the entity responsible for the haunting claimed kinship with Satan himself!

Matthew Hopkins.

It started in November 1654 in a house in the Scottish village of Glenluce. The household consisted of Gilbert Campbell, a weaver; his wife, Grizel; their children; and a servant named Margaret.

At first, inside and outside the house, there were sounds like shrill whistles. Then Janet, one of Gilbert's daughters, and another woman were visiting a well when they heard the whistling sound and a voice like Janet's threatening to cast her into the well.

Soon after, the poltergeist started throwing stones through windows, doors, and down the chimney. The threads of Gilbert's loom were cut, and the family would see their hats, clothes, and shoes slashed—even while they were still wearing them. It tore blankets from the beds and scattered the contents of chests and trunks, concealing tools in tiny holes and cracks. The situation worsened so much that the weaver had to take his tools to a neighbour's house. Some of the neighbours thought the activity was centred on one of the children, so they were sent away for five days. During their absence, the phenomenon ceased.

One by one, the children were sent home. However, nothing happened until one of them, Thomas, returned. With his arrival, fires broke out around the building. It was decided to send the boy to the parish minister, the Reverend John Scott. Despite this, the activity continued in the family home. Clothes vanished or were found slashed. The poltergeist pelted the farm with peat and pulled turf off the roof and walls. It also resorted to attacking the family with pins that left bloody marks on their skin. Thomas heard a voice instructing him not to enter the building upon his return. This warning was ignored, and the boy was attacked, forcing his return to the Reverend Scott.

The voice then began to engage in hours of conversation with the whole family. Reverend Scott, bringing witnesses to the house—including his wife and several gentlemen—all heard it address them in Latin or Lowland Scots. The entity claimed to be the son of Satan and told them the names of "the witches of Glenluce." When it was pointed out that one of the women it had named was dead, the voice replied, "It is true she is dead long ago, but her spirit is living with us in the world." It also threatened to set the roof on fire if Thomas Campbell did not leave and asked for a shovel to dig its grave. It claimed that Christ had given it a written commission to torment the family, accused another witness, Robert Hay, of being a witch, and mocked another man for wearing a broad-rimmed hat. It claimed to live in the "bottomless pit of hell" and demanded in a loud voice that all the candles be extinguished so it could appear to them as a ball of fire. So powerful was this noise that the witnesses said it sounded as though the voice were shouting in their ears.

Once, it asked for oatcakes as it was hungry and requested a belt to bind its bones together. At times, it was noted that the voice appeared to come from under a bed, outside the house, or from the children themselves while lying in bed. On a more sinister note, it threatened to dash out the brains of one of the children. However, the family had become so familiar with the poltergeist that the girl dismissed the threat and returned to her work.

The poltergeist also appeared as a naked hand and arm, beating on the floor with such force that the house shook. This was followed by the alarming cry, "Come up, my father; come up. I will send my father among you; see there, he is behind your backs."

At this point, the minister claimed to have seen another hand and arm, which the poltergeist said belonged to his father, the Devil, as the palm was blacker. The entity also predicted that it would remain after the minister's death—an accurate prediction, as Reverend Scott died in December of that same year.

When the witnesses prepared to leave, the poltergeist boasted that it would beat the children or burn down the house. However, it failed to carry out either threat.

After six months, the activity stopped. But four months later, in July 1655, the poltergeist returned with new assaults and the destruction of the family's food—an act that left them almost starving. In October, the Synod, the regional body of presbyteries, was approached by Gilbert Campbell and asked for help. However, it was not until February 1656 that they finally met in Glenluce and decided to implore God to help the family and declare a day of fasting in southwest Scotland. Coincidence or not, the paranormal activity started to decline, and by April, it had ceased. However, four months later, the poltergeist returned. It stole food from the table and concealed it around the house or outside. Once, while Grizel was preparing breakfast, it snatched a plate from her. She calmly requested the plate's return, only to have it flung back at her. In September, the poltergeist's attempts to disrupt the family intensified, with stones falling on the house and members of the household attacked in their beds by wooden staves. A voice was heard shouting that it would burn the house down. It attempted to carry out this threat by setting fire to a bed, but the fire was stopped before it took hold. Perhaps this failed attempt discouraged the poltergeist, for the 'Devil of Glenluce,' as it had become known, was never heard from again.

It was recorded at the time that a beggar named Alexander Agnew had threatened to harm the family because they had refused his request for alms. While some believed he used witchcraft to cause the phenomenon, the records reveal his execution for blasphemy in May 1656—several weeks before the poltergeist finally ceased its activities.

Unfortunately, we do not know the Campbells' situation at the time of the poltergeist's first appearance or how many children were living in the house, nor do we know their ages. Judging by accounts written at the time, the boy Thomas or his sister Janet may have been the focus of the haunting, but lacking further information, we can never know for sure. Despite this, the haunting must be considered one of the most fascinating examples of poltergeist activity ever recorded in the British Isles.

A few years later, another poltergeist outbreak occurred in Galashiels, on the Scottish border. Although the Devil was blamed, it is noteworthy as it was also linked at the time to possible sexual activity in the girl's home. The victim, a young girl of twelve or thirteen named Margaret Wilson, had been disturbed by scratching sounds coming from her bed and noises like a rasping iron that appeared to come from her chest. Her body would also levitate. Attempts by several strong men to hold her down proved impossible. She was also pulled up and down by her feet and claimed that the Devil had spoken to her and offered her gifts. On another occasion, she said he appeared to her as a man and asked her not to attend church.

The child eventually moved to Edinburgh, and the phenomenon ceased. The local minister, the Reverend Wilkie, appeared to be very perceptive, for he took the girl's uncle for a midnight walk soon after the events had occurred and asked him to reflect on his ways and consider if he had done anything to anger God. He then spoke of local gossip and accused him of something, which the man immediately denied. Upon close examination, it seems that there were hints of the uncle harbouring incestuous intentions towards the girl. The minister appeared to establish a connection between the poltergeist activity and the uncle's potential sexual interest in his niece. Regardless of the situation, it is intriguing to observe that the poltergeist disappeared once the girl left the household and was beyond her uncle's reach.

The link between witchcraft, black magic, and poltergeist activity runs deep through the historical record, especially during times of fear, social unrest, and religious upheaval. In the 17th century, when the Glenluce poltergeist declared itself a son of Satan and began naming witches, it merely echoed the anxieties of a society obsessed with the Devil's supposed reach into everyday life. For many, mysterious knockings, flying stones, or levitating girls could only be explained through the lens of supernatural persecution—often blamed on witches, demons, or divine punishment.

But as the cases of Thomas Campbell and Margaret Wilson reveal, these hauntings were not just religious or superstitious experiences; they were deeply personal.

They revolved around households, family tensions, and sometimes—as with Margaret—disturbing and possibly repressed realities no one dared speak aloud. That a 17th-century minister might have intuited a link between paranormal disturbances and the sexual dynamics within a home is a sobering insight, especially considering that modern theories now regularly associate poltergeist phenomena with psychological stress, trauma, or adolescence.

Still, in the minds of those who lived through these terrifying episodes, the cause was often clear: witchcraft, the Devil, or the lingering wrath of those wronged by society. Whether these manifestations were the result of spiritual assault or unconscious psychological projection, one truth remains—poltergeist outbreaks of this era were rarely random. They struck where fear, secrecy, and shame already existed, often leaving destruction in their wake and, just as mysteriously, vanishing when the human source of tension was removed.

The Devil may have had many names, but he often seemed to know exactly whose house to visit.

Chapter Six

The Drummer of Tedworth

Belief in witchcraft and sorcery continued to influence interpretations of unexplained phenomena well into the 17th century. One of the most prominent cases occurred in England just two years after the restoration of the monarchy. In March 1662, John Mompesson, a landowner and magistrate, was visiting Ludgershall in Wiltshire when he was disturbed by persistent street drumming. He discovered the noise was caused by William Drury, an itinerant vagrant and self-proclaimed conjurer.

Drury had served in the Parliamentarian army during the English Civil War but also claimed to have fought for Charles I. Mompesson discovered that Drury had forged a permit to beg and subsequently

The Phantom Drummer.

had him arrested. He promised Drury that if he could prove his honesty, he would be released and his drum returned. Drury was eventually released but did not recover the drum, which by then had been sent to Mompesson's residence in Tedworth, Wiltshire.

When Mompesson returned home, his wife told him that she had heard loud noises outside the house. Terrified, she thought that several thieves were trying to break in. Mompesson also heard these sounds and rushed out, armed with a pistol, but could find no one. The sounds continued, eventually entering the house and moving to the room where the drum was kept.

Interestingly, the disturbances stopped when Mrs. Mompesson went into labour. The poltergeist remained quiet for three weeks. When the sounds resumed, the activity focused on the children. The children's rooms would resound with military drumbeats, and their beds would occasionally tremble so violently that it was feared they would collapse. The children heard scratching under the beds, and these noises followed them around the house. There were also glimpses of small, shimmering blue lights. The poltergeist would pull blankets off the beds and open and close doors. A sound like a rustling silk dress was also heard.

Once, a servant saw a wooden board move and jokingly asked the spirit to give it to him. The board floated up to his hand, but the poltergeist refused to let go, resulting in a tug of war that lasted for some twenty minutes until Mompesson ordered them to stop. Following this, the house smelled of sulphur. A minister came to pray with the children, and the noises retreated to an attic. When the praying ended, the noises returned to the room. Chairs began to move, and the children's shoes and other objects were thrown over their heads. A bedstaff was then thrown at the minister, hitting him in the leg—but, according to an account of the time, "hit him so favourably, that a lock of wool could not have fallen more softly."

Mompesson decided to take the children to a neighbour's house. However, his ten-year-old daughter was placed in her father's bed, where, according to a contemporary report, "the disturbance began there again, continuing three weeks, drumming and making other noises, and it was observed that it would answer exactly, in drumming, anything that was beaten or called for."

The sounds were now loud enough to be heard in the fields around the house. The poltergeist also had a sense of humour. Mompesson's mother said that the phantom drummer should leave them money to make up for all the trouble it had caused.

The next night, the sound of chinking money was heard all over the house. However, its humour could also take a darker turn. On one occasion, Mompesson went into his stable and found his horse on its back, with its hind hoof stuck firmly in its mouth; it had to be pried out by several men using a lever. A blacksmith, who had heard about the haunting but was sceptical, visited the house and heard noises like the shoeing of a horse and pincers that sounded as if they were snapping at his nose. Later, a panting dog was heard, and a woman carrying a staff had it snatched from her hand. One unheated room was suddenly filled with "a bloomy, noisome smell" and became hot, despite it being cold outside.

King Charles II took an interest in the case and sent two of his courtiers—Philip Stanhope, 2nd Earl of Chesterfield, and Charles Berkeley, Earl of Falmouth—to investigate the reported haunting. However, the manifestations ceased during their visit and resumed only after they had left, frustrating any conclusive observation.

This outcome did little to dampen Charles's curiosity. His interest in the occult was pragmatic rather than devotional; he approached supernatural phenomena with a blend of scepticism and curiosity, as reflected in various historical accounts.

Later, the King reportedly claimed that Mompesson had privately admitted the haunting was a hoax—an assertion Mompesson firmly denied.

The poltergeist reportedly turned more violent after the two earls left, beating the children's legs until they were completely black and blue. Once, it placed a long spike in Mompesson's bed and a knife in his mother's. It filled bowls with ashes, hid a Bible in the grate, and turned the money in people's pockets black. It was even heard purring, like a cat. On one occasion, a servant claimed to have seen, at the foot of their bed, "a great body with two red and glaring eyes, which, for some time, were fixed steadily on him, and at length disappeared."

Attempts were made to communicate with the entity. Mompesson suspected William Drury was responsible and asked the poltergeist if this was so: "Satan, if the drummer set thee to work, give three knocks and no more." Three knocks were heard in reply. Next, Mompesson asked for five knocks to confirm Drury's involvement. Five knocks were heard. By now, Mompesson had burnt Drury's drum in a nearby field. But despite this, the haunting continued.

Knocks, scratches, thumps, and panting continued to plague the house. A voice was also heard chanting "A witch, a witch!" over a hundred times, and marks like a great claw, letters of the alphabet, and circles were seen in ashes spread across the floor. Mompesson fired at a moving piece of wood. Later, he found spots of blood on the hearth and stairs.

The Reverend Joseph Glanvill, who later wrote about the case, visited Mompesson's home and heard a dog panting and strange scratching sounds around the children's beds. Glanvill also saw something moving in a linen bag hanging by a bed. He assumed it was a rat or mouse but discovered the bag was empty. He later went to collect his horse and found it sweating in terror. It died not long afterwards.

In 1663, William Drury was arrested in Gloucester for pig stealing. He was found guilty and was ordered to be transported, but he escaped from the barge sent to take him to the ship. Prior to his escape, he

Joseph Glanvill.

The Demon Drummer of Tedworth.

reportedly asked a prison visitor about the news from Wiltshire and then spoke of the phantom drummer in Tedworth. He boasted that he had caused the disturbances: "I have plagued him, and he'll never be quiet until he has made me satisfaction for taking away my drum." Drury also said he had learnt magic from "gallant books he had of a wizard" in Oliver Cromwell's New Model Army.

Mompesson came to hear of Drury's escape and his claim of causing the drumming. He had him arrested and accused of witchcraft, a capital crime at the time. In August 1663, the court in Salisbury heard the case. Surprisingly, Drury was acquitted. However, the court, aware of his earlier conviction and escape, again ordered his transportation out of the country. What happened to Drury after he left England is unknown. Following Drury's final departure, the disturbances reportedly ceased. Mompesson claimed his home had been quiet ever since.

The case of the Tedworth Drummer stands as one of the earliest and most thoroughly documented poltergeist accounts in English history. Yet, despite the involvement of magistrates, clergy, nobles, and even royal courtiers, it remains as puzzling now as it must have seemed in the 1660s. Was William Drury truly the malevolent force behind the disturbances, using sorcery learned from wartime comrades? Or was he simply a convenient scapegoat in an age when fear of witchcraft and the Devil still gripped the public imagination?

At its heart, the haunting at Tedworth reveals the complex intersection between personal grievance, political turmoil, and lingering superstition. Just as England was struggling to re-establish order following civil war, regicide and republican rule, a spectral drumbeat began pounding through the home of a man who represented the rule of law. That this haunting appeared to be sparked by a confrontation between a landowner and a vagrant is no coincidence. It echoed wider social anxieties about authority, class, and the consequences of displacement in a changing world.

Whether one sees the poltergeist as a supernatural tormentor, a psychological manifestation of stress and guilt, or the work of cunning human deception, the case remains a powerful reminder of how deeply belief in witchcraft and black magic shaped the experiences—and explanations—of people in early modern

Britain. The phantom drummer may have fallen silent, but his story continues to reverberate through centuries of folklore and debate.

Chapter Seven

The Epworth Rectory Haunting

As Britain entered the 18th century and the Age of Enlightenment, attitudes toward witchcraft began to shift. John Wesley, founder of the Methodist movement, lamented this change, writing: "The English in general, and indeed most of the men of learning in Europe, have given up all accounts of witches and apparitions as mere old wives' fables." He added, "I am sorry for it," believing that abandoning belief in witchcraft was "in effect giving up the Bible."

Wesley's frustration may have been influenced by a personal connection to the supernatural. Between December 1716 and January 1717, his father's rectory in Epworth, Lincolnshire, was reportedly haunted by a poltergeist. At first, the nights were filled with groans and knocks. Soon after, the family heard jingling coins, breaking glass, and footsteps racing up and down the stairs—often so loud they caused the entire house to shake. The family mastiff reacted with visible terror.

One of John's sisters, Hetty, claimed to have heard an apparition on the stairs: "something like a man in a loose nightgown trailing after him."

Her sister Molly also had a frightening encounter. While reading in the dining room, she heard a door open—though it remained closed—and then sensed someone walking around her. Terrified, she fled upstairs to her mother's room. On another occasion, a headless badger was seen under a bed and later spotted sitting by the dining-room fire by Robert Brown, a servant. The creature was then seen running through the hall, but a search of the house revealed nothing. A white rabbit was also reportedly seen in the kitchen. The presence became so familiar that Emily, another sister, nicknamed it "Old Jeffrey," after an elderly man who had died in the house.

Emily believed the ghost was the result of witchcraft. In a letter to her brother Samuel in London, she speculated that their father's condemnation of "cunning men" in his sermons had provoked one of them to retaliate by conjuring a spirit to haunt the family.

John Wesley.

Epworth Rectory.
Photo by John West.

Samuel Wesley, John's father, kept a journal of the events. He recorded his servant hearing a noise like a gobbling turkey in the garret and described being pushed out of his study by "an invisible power". He also noted that whenever he prayed for King George I and the Prince of Wales, knocking sounds would occur—prompting some family members to joke that the spirit was a Jacobite.

Attempts were made to communicate with the entity. Concerned that the disturbances were an omen of his son Samuel's death, Wesley senior asked the spirit to knock if it were Samuel. There was no response. On another occasion, Mrs. Wesley tapped her foot on the floor, and the poltergeist mimicked the taps beneath her feet. Friends urged the family to leave the rectory, but Samuel Wesley refused. By January 1717, the phenomenon had ceased. Old Jeffrey never returned.

Some researchers have speculated that the Wesleys were victims of a plot to drive them out. Samuel Wesley was unpopular in the parish, partly due to his rigid personality. For example, he reportedly left a previous parish in anger after the squire's mistress spoke to his wife, Susanna. He also once left his family for a year because his wife refused to pray for King George. Some believe that a fire in 1709—which nearly killed young John—may have been arson. Could the ghostly events have been a coordinated effort by disgruntled townsfolk to force the family out?

Some cast a shadow of doubt over nineteen-year-old Hetty, suspecting her of orchestrating the disturbances herself. Whispers of suspicion grew louder when it was claimed she alone, among all the family, left no written account of the haunting. Yet this silence may not have been what it seemed. In a surviving letter to their brother Samuel, her sister Suky made reference to a now-lost letter from Hetty— one that spoke of the ghostly events that had shaken their home.

Hetty appeared to be the focal point of the activity. Before the noises began, she often trembled in her sleep, and the sounds seemed to follow her. Her mother wrote, "It was commonly nearer her than the rest." Another sister noted, "The noise never followed me as it did my sister Hetty. I have been with her when it has knocked under her, and when she moved, it has followed her and still kept just under her feet."

The Epworth case lacks some elements typically associated with poltergeist phenomena—there was no stone-throwing, no apports, and no objects hurled through the air, although door latches were observed to move and the handle of a mill was once seen to "turn round with great swiftness."

Could Hetty or someone outside the household have faked the events? It seems unlikely. The sounds—knocks, crashes, and bangs—occurred in multiple rooms, responded to foot taps, and retreated when pursued by Hetty's youngest sister, Kezzy. What explains the invisible turkey heard in the garret, the headless badger, or the phantom white rabbit seen by witnesses? If this were a hoax, why did it stop so suddenly after a few weeks?

We can only speculate on Hetty's mental state during the period, or on the emotional climate of the Wesley household. Some theories suggest that the poltergeist may have manifested as a result of suppressed psychological tensions. Hetty, known for her interest in male companionship, later became pregnant out of wedlock. The arrival of Robert Brown at the rectory may have stirred repressed desires that emerged through poltergeist activity.

Other interpretations point to Mrs. Wesley. The poltergeists's apparent hostility to King George could indicate it was influenced by her. Her relationship with her husband was challenging, and her frequent pregnancies, political disagreements, and Samuel's temporary abandonment of her could have created deep-seated resentment. Notably, Samuel recorded being violently pushed by the poltergeist on three separate occasions. Could these have been physical manifestations of his wife's subconscious anger?

While John Wesley held fast to his belief in spirits—arguing that disbelief in witchcraft was akin to disbelief in the Bible—many Enlightenment thinkers disagreed.

Ghosts and poltergeists, they argued, were illusions, hysteria, or fraud. The Epworth poltergeist, however, remains one of the more detailed and intriguing accounts of a haunting during a period that was supposed to be ruled by reason.

The Epworth case is a curious blend of personal, spiritual, and cultural tensions. Whether the result of fraud, family stress, or a genuine unexplained phenomenon, it demonstrates that even in an age committed to science and scepticism, belief in the supernatural continued to find fertile ground. For the Wesley family—especially John—it was a reminder that forces beyond human understanding might still linger at the edges of reason.

Chapter Eight
The Cock Lane Haunting

Another 18th-century haunting, the Cock Lane ghost, was thought by many to be a hoax. Indeed, William Hogarth, one of the greatest painters and satirists of the time, mocked the incident in his print *Credulity, Superstition and Fanaticism*, which depicted members of a church congregation clutching statues of the Cock Lane ghost. One man is even shown pushing a statue of the ghost down a lady's bodice, who appears to be in the throes of religious—and apparent sexual—ecstasy.

William Hogarth's Credulity, Superstition, and Fanaticism.

The story began when William Kent moved to London with Fanny Lynes, the sister of his deceased wife, whom he claimed was now his spouse. In 1760, the couple lodged with Mr. and Mrs. Richard Parsons in Cock Lane. While Kent was away at a wedding, he asked the Parsons' eleven-year-old daughter, Elizabeth, to stay with Fanny. During his absence, strange scratchings and knockings were heard behind the wainscot in their room. Mrs. Parsons first suggested the noises came from a cobbler next door, but this was dismissed when the sounds continued on a Sunday—when the cobbler did not work.

By this time, Fanny was pregnant. Kent admitted to the landlord that they were not married and demanded repayment of a loan he had given to Parsons. When Parsons refused, Kent took legal action.

After the couple moved out, Fanny died of smallpox and was buried in the crypt of St. John's Church in Clerkenwell. Yet the strange noises continued at their former lodgings, especially in Elizabeth's room. Parsons and a local publican claimed to see a white figure in the house, which they assumed was Fanny's ghost. Notable figures like the Duke of York and Horace Walpole, the writer and Whig politician, visited the house, hoping to witness the supernatural events firsthand. Among the oddities occuring at this time was a whirring noise likened to the sound of a large bird flapping through the room.

Events now took a sinister turn, with the entity accusing Kent—via raps in answer to questions—that he had poisoned Fanny to claim her money. Another message said that Kent should hang. Kent, hearing of the allegations, confronted Parsons and demanded a retraction. Kent was then invited to Cock Lane to question the ghost. He agreed and thoroughly searched the room for any signs of trickery. At first, the ghost was quiet, but then, in response to questions put to it by Reverend John Moore, it repeated the

Cock Lane.

claim that she had been murdered. Kent denounced the spirit, crying, "Thou art not the ghost of my Fanny. She would never have said any such thing."

A committee was formed to investigate the case, including the famed Dr. Samuel Johnson, who later wrote an account of what had happened.

"About ten at night the gentlemen met in the chamber in which the girl, supposed to be disturbed by a spirit, had with proper caution been put to bed by several ladies. They sat rather more than one hour, and hearing nothing, went down-stairs, where they interrogated the father of the girl, who denied in the strongest terms any knowledge or belief of fraud. While they were enquiring and deliberating, they were summoned into the girl's chamber by some ladies who were near her bed and who had heard knocks and scratches. When the gentlemen entered, the girl declared that she felt the spirit like a mouse upon her back, when the spirit was very solemnly required to manifest its existence by appearance, by impression on the hand or body of any present, or any other agency, but no evidence of any preternatural power was exhibited. The spirit was then very seriously advertised that the person to whom the promise was made of striking the coffin was then about to visit the vault, and that the performance of the promise was then claimed. The company at one o'clock went into the church, and the gentlemen to whom the promise was made went with another into the vault. The spirit was solemnly required to perform its promise, but nothing more than silence ensued. The person supposed to be the accused by the spirit [Kent] then went down with several others, but no effort was perceived. Upon their return, they examined the girl but could draw no confession from her. Between two and three, she desired and was permitted to go home with her father. It is therefore the opinion of the whole assembly that the child has some art of making or counterfeiting a particular noise and that there is no agency of any higher cause."

It was made clear to Elizabeth that if the ghost did not materialise, she, her mother, and her father would be sent to Newgate Prison. The servants were instructed to spy on the girl through a crack in the door. It was not long before they saw her take a piece of wood and hide it in her bed. Later, as a crowd gathered in the room, scratching and knocking noises were heard coming from Elizabeth's bed. However, these sounds differed from the earlier ones, and a search of the bed revealed the wooden board. It appeared that Dr. Johnson had been correct in his belief that the ghost was a hoax.

Kent sued Parsons, his wife, and Mary Fraser (a friend acting as Elizabeth's chaperone and 'questioner') for conspiracy to slander. The jury took only 15 minutes to find them guilty. Parsons was sentenced to two years in prison and ordered to stand in the pillory three times in one month. His wife received one year, and Fraser six months. Reverend John Moore and an associate were ordered to pay damages.

Today, people frequently cite the Cock Lane ghost as a classic hoax. But was it? Many aspects of this case suggest that not all the phenomena were faked. Clearly, Elizabeth was the focus of the haunting. Observers saw her shiver and tremble when the knocking began. They also heard whispering noises around the girl's bed, but upon placing a candle near her lips, they found them closed. Even after a maid holding Elizabeth's hands and feet remained in bed with her, the rapping and scratching noises persisted. Yes, a board had later been found hidden in Elizabeth's bed, but this was only after the girl had been frightened by the threat that she and her family would be thrown into prison if the ghost failed to do something. So was a poltergeist responsible after all? We know little of Elizabeth's emotional and mental state at the time of the

Plan of the Room, and the GHOST's Reprefentations, with References.

manifestations, but it would be churlish to dismiss all the events at Cock Lane as fraud and trickery.

And what of the claim that Fanny Lynes had been murdered? There is an intriguing postscript to this story. In 1844, J. W. Archer, an artist, paid a visit to the crypt where Fanny had been laid to rest.

"The place was at the time in great confusion, with coffins, remains of bodies, some of which were dried like mummies, etc. I could find no better seat than one of the coffins. The sexton's boy, who held my light, informed me that this was the coffin of Scratching Fanny, which recalled the Cock Lane ghost to my mind. I got off the lid of the coffin and saw the face of a handsome woman with an aquiline nose; this feature remaining perfect, an uncommon case for the cartilage, mostly gives away. The remains had become adipocere [a waxy substance formed by the decomposition of soft tissue] and were perfectly preserved. She was said to have been poisoned by deleterious punch, but this was legally disproved, and, if I remember rightly, she was otherwise declared to have died of smallpox. Of this disease there was not the least sign; but as some mineral poisons tend to render the body adipocere, here was some evidence in support of the former allegation. I made particular enquiries of Mr. Bird, churchwarden, a respectable and judicious man; and he gave me good assurance that this coffin had always been looked upon as the one containing the Cock Lane woman."

A case that bears many striking similarities to the Cock Lane haunting took place over a century later in April 1864, in Scott's Lane, Port Glasgow. The family in residence heard persistent knocking between 7 and 10 p.m., drawing large crowds.

Things became so bad that the local police were brought in to keep the peace. Sergeant James MacDonald received a suggestion from Andrew Glendinning, a resident of Port Glasgow, to investigate the matter. The first sounds resembled scratching on rough boards. Knocks like the sound of a hammer were then heard under a bed. It was found that the knocks were replying to questions in the affirmative or negative— three knocks for yes and one for

Visiting the Church Crypt.

no. Occasionally, the answer would come before the question concluded. Glendinning thought that some of the knocks resembled the tune *"There is nae luck about the house."* He started to whistle the tune, which resulted in the knocks becoming louder and accompanying the whistling. As Glendinning whistled other popular Scottish tunes, the knocks always joined in on the second line, consistently matching the exact timing of the chosen tune. At times, the knocks accompanied the striking of the town clock.

Small objects, including coal and potatoes, were found scattered around the property, and a hand was seen moving up and down behind a bed—always vanishing before it could be caught., leaving a trace of cold air.

Part of the floor was removed in an attempt to pinpoint the precise nature of the knocks. At times, it was noted that the knocks appeared to be coming from the very edge of a hole that had been made in the floor. The rest of the house was examined, including the lobby, staircase, cellars, and children's beds, but nothing was found to account for the sounds. Attempts were even made to reproduce them by knocking on various places around the house, but these sounded nothing like the knocks made by the poltergeist. The strange activity eventually ceased, but it left behind more questions than answers. The suspected hoax was never proven.

While belief in witchcraft waned throughout the 18th century, hauntings like those at Cock Lane continued to spark fascination—and controversy. For some, these events confirmed long-held beliefs about the dead lingering among the living. For others, they provided cautionary tales about credulity and fraud.

Yet even as Enlightenment thinking dismissed such phenomena as superstition or trickery, the 19th century ushered in a new era of interest in the supernatural. The rise of Spiritualism—with its séances, spirit mediums, and ghostly communications—can be seen as a direct descendant of cases like the Cock Lane ghost. These earlier hauntings provided a cultural and psychological foundation upon which Spiritualism would build. Victorians, captivated by both science and the spirit world, were ready to believe again—not in witches, but in the souls of the departed, eager to speak from beyond.

Chapter Nine

The Outsider Investigates: Colin Wilson and the Poltergeist Enigma

Although poltergeists have fascinated occult researchers and writers for well over a century, one of the most respected figures in the field of paranormal studies must surely be Colin Wilson—the noted author, philosopher, and self-described "existentialist outsider" who rose to fame with the publication of *The Outsider* in 1956.

While *The Outsider* dealt with themes of alienation and the search for meaning, Wilson's later work expanded into the realms of consciousness, mysticism, and the unexplained.

Wilson became deeply interested in poltergeists while researching material for his book *The Occult*, a work that did much to legitimise serious discussion of paranormal phenomena. He brought a level of intellectual rigor, literary flair, and philosophical depth rarely found in the field, helping to ensure that topics like poltergeists were treated not as tabloid sensationalism, but as subjects worthy of thoughtful exploration.

Initially approaching the subject with scepticism, Wilson soon found a wealth of evidence suggesting that there was far more to ghosts, extrasensory perception (ESP), and poltergeists than simple trickery or fraud. He also recalled a personal experience from 1960, when a poltergeist outbreak occurred in his Cornwall home after his father, mother, and thirteen-year-old sister came to live with him and his family.

Colin Wilson.
Photo: Colin Wilson Estate.

One sunny morning, Wilson was awakened by a loud, repeated banging—similar to someone hammering on metal. At first, he assumed a bed had collapsed in the attic, where two friends were staying. He called up to them, but there was no reply.

Upon checking, he found both friends still asleep. He also glanced into his sister's room and saw that she, too, was sleeping. The noises persisted, now seeming to come from outside the house—perhaps from the roof.

Wilson went outside and walked around the building but could not locate the sound, although it appeared to be coming from overhead. However, a check of the hot water pipes revealed that it was not coming from them. His father joined him, but they were still unable to pinpoint the noise. As it was 5 a.m., they decided to return to bed, but ten minutes later, the banging started again—although this time briefly. The sounds never returned, and Wilson theorised that his sister was somehow responsible, as she was unhappy about having to leave Leicester and move to the countryside.

Because of this personal experience, Wilson became convinced that poltergeists were caused by the psychic sexual energy of a troubled mind—usually an adolescent—a force able to manifest itself by moving objects and generally causing mayhem in the young person's home. After all, had not Sigmund Freud argued that the unconscious mind is an ocean of dangerous currents? Indeed, he also emphasised that the most powerful force is the sex drive.

One famous poltergeist case that intrigued Wilson occurred in Rosenheim, Bavaria. The poltergeist appeared to be linked to a 19-year-old secretary, Annemarie Schaberl, who worked in a solicitor's office. The haunting began in the autumn of 1967. Light fittings would explode or swing back and forth. Fuses would blow—a specially installed meter revealed sudden, unexplained surges of power—and heavy office furniture moved on its own. A framed painting revolved around its hook, and fluid was found leaking from the office copier. Additionally, someone made numerous outgoing calls to the "speaking clock" service, dialling the number 40 to 50 times in a row. The employees denied making the calls.

The case was investigated by Hans Bender, a German parapsychologist. He noted that Annemarie Schaberl was always present when the poltergeist activity occurred. For example, whenever she walked down the hall, light fixtures would swing behind her, and the power surges only happened when she was in the office. Bender also found that the phone system simultaneously registered four dials for a nine-digit Munich number—something that would require mechanical influence on specific springs at millisecond time intervals. He installed electronic monitoring equipment and measured large power supply deflections in conjunction with the poltergeist phenomenon. These deflections occurred only during office hours. Interestingly, a battery registered 3 volts instead of 1.5 volts, suggesting that the poltergeist generated an electric current.

Bender spoke to Schaberl, who admitted that she hated living in the town and disliked her job. Her family life had been difficult, as her father was a rigid disciplinarian, and although she was engaged, her emotional life was unsatisfactory. In 1968, the poltergeist activity at the office ceased when Schaberl left her job and joined another workplace. However, the phenomenon continued to plague her.

Her engagement ended after her boyfriend took her to a bowling alley, where he witnessed the pin-setting system and electronic scoring suddenly malfunction.

After she began working at a mill, a man was killed in an accident, and people there started to avoid her. Eventually, she married someone else and had three children. From that point on, the poltergeist no longer troubled her.

During his study of the poltergeist phenomenon, Wilson was also reminded of an event mentioned by Carl Jung, the Swiss psychiatrist and psychoanalyst. Jung's female cousin had begun to go into trances at the age of puberty and spoke in strange voices. But that was not all—a table suddenly split apart, and a sideboard was rocked by an explosion. Inside, a knife was found shattered into several pieces.

Jung coined the term "exteriorisation phenomenon" and was convinced that the girl's unconscious mind was responsible.

Sigmund Freud, Jung's friend and colleague, remained unconvinced, leading to an argument between the two. Jung, irritated by Freud's scepticism, felt a burning sensation in his chest, as if his diaphragm were becoming red hot. Suddenly, the pair heard a loud explosion coming from the bookcase. "There," said Jung, "that was an exteriorisation phenomenon." "Bosh," replied Freud, to which Jung said, "It is not bosh, and to prove it, there will be another explosion in a moment." A second explosion quickly occurred. Jung was convinced that his anger had caused both sounds.

However, Wilson also noted that Harry Price—best remembered today for his investigation of the alleged haunting at Borley Rectory in Essex—did not entirely agree with the belief that poltergeists were solely the product of a troubled teenage mind. In his book *Poltergeist Over England*, Price stated that he believed them to be "invisible, intangible, malicious, and noisy entities," adding that "poltergeists are able, by laws yet unknown to our physicists, to extract energy from living persons, often from the young and usually from girl adolescents, especially if they suffer from some mental disorder."

Nevertheless, Price did acknowledge that poltergeists appeared to be connected to sexual energy, recalling that the husband of Austrian medium

Frieda Weisl had once told him that during their early years of marriage, objects would suddenly jump off shelves when she orgasmed. On one occasion, all the pots and pans in their kitchen began dancing around the room during her sexual climax. However, during her periods, no phenomena would occur, and during séances, she was unable to make contact with spirits.

Colin Wilson's exploration of poltergeist phenomena marked a turning point in how such disturbances were viewed. By drawing on personal experience, historical accounts, and the ideas of thinkers like Freud and Jung, Wilson reframed the poltergeist as a manifestation of the unconscious mind—a force not just destructive, but revealing. In doing so, he challenged both the hardened sceptics who dismissed all such activity as fraud and the spiritualists who saw it purely as evidence of discarnate entities.

Cases like Rosenheim and the strange outbreaks tied to adolescent turmoil offered compelling, if unsettling, evidence for his theory: that the energy unleashed during emotional or sexual repression might externalise itself in physical ways—disrupting technology, moving objects, or even causing harm. Yet even as Wilson promoted this idea, he did not ignore the darker possibility hinted at by researchers like Harry Price—that some poltergeists may, in fact, be independent and intelligent forces, capable of drawing energy from the living and operating by laws science has yet to comprehend.

Chapter Ten

The Split Brain

Colin Wilson was aware that the human brain consists of two halves connected by a bridge of nerve fibres known as the corpus callosum. The two halves of the brain appear to have different functions. For example, a man with damage to the left brain has trouble expressing himself in words, while a man with damage to the right brain can still speak clearly but has difficulty drawing simple patterns. In short, the left hemisphere deals with speech and logic, while the right deals with recognition and intuition. To quote Wilson: "The left brain is a scientist; the right is the artist."

He also noted that, in the 1930s, it was discovered that people suffering from epilepsy could be cured if the bridge of nerve fibres was severed. Oddly, this operation seemed to make no major difference to the patients' everyday lives.

In the 1950s, Roger Sperry of the University of Chicago found that these 'splitbrain' patients appeared to turn into two people. For instance, one patient tried to embrace his wife with one hand, only to find his other hand pushing her away. Another patient was shown a picture of an orange with his right eye and an apple with his left. He was then asked to write with his left hand what he had just seen, and he wrote "apple." Asked what he had written, he replied, "orange."

It was as if, as Wilson observed, we have two people living in the two halves of our brain. The person we call 'I' lives in the left brain, while the person living in the right brain could almost be described as a stranger. And does the right brain, Wilson wondered, possess the powers of psychokinesis—something that the poltergeist uses to manifest itself?

Colin Wilson had met several individuals who claimed to possess telekinetic powers, among whom Uri Geller stood out as one of the most famous and controversial figures. Geller, an Israeli-born performer and self-proclaimed psychic, rose to international prominence in the 1970s for his seemingly extraordinary ability to bend spoons and keys simply by gently rubbing them with his finger or focusing his concentration. Beyond these feats, he could also snap metal rings by hovering his hand above them without any physical contact. His performances often blurred the lines between stage magic and genuine psychic phenomena, captivating both the public and some members of the scientific community.

Wilson was impressed by Geller's abilities, especially given the numerous occasions on which Geller appeared to reproduce phenomena traditionally associated with poltergeists—such as objects moving or bending inexplicably in the presence of witnesses. Geller's demonstrations sparked a wave of scientific interest, leading to controlled experiments designed to test the reality of his powers under laboratory conditions.

One notable test took place in September 1974 at London University, involving physicists John Hasted, David Bohm, and Ted Bastin—respected scientists who were willing to explore the possibility of psychic phenomena with an open mind. During this experiment, a small circular piece of vanadium foil, used in electron microscopy, was sealed inside a plastic capsule. One of the scientists placed his hand over the capsule, followed by Geller placing his hand on top. When the capsule was later examined, a portion of the foil had mysteriously disappeared, suggesting that Geller had somehow disintegrated part of the metal through psychokinesis.

Uri Geller.
Photo: Jason Figgis.

On another occasion, Geller bent an aluminum disc that had been sealed in a plastic container, an action that seemed impossible without direct physical manipulation. Perhaps even more astonishingly, a piece of brass located across the laboratory spontaneously bent and then flew across the room, landing near the door without any apparent cause. These occurrences fueled intense debate about the legitimacy of Geller's abilities and the potential existence of forces or energies beyond current scientific understanding.

Despite the compelling nature of these demonstrations, Geller's claims and performances were met with scepticism and accusations of trickery by some members of the scientific community and professional magicians alike. Critics argued that his feats could be replicated through sleight of hand or cleverly concealed gimmicks. Nevertheless, Geller inspired a generation of researchers, including Colin Wilson, to seriously consider the possibility that human consciousness might wield untapped powers capable of influencing the physical world. Whether genuine or illusory, Geller's feats remain some of the most debated examples of telekinesis and continue to provoke curiosity about the mysterious capacities of the human mind.

Another person who reportedly demonstrated the ability to manipulate objects through apparent thought alone was Nina Kulagina, a Russian woman who gained international attention during the Cold War for her alleged psychokinetic powers. Born in 1926 in Leningrad (now St. Petersburg), Kulagina first attracted scientific interest in the 1960s, when Soviet researchers began to study her unusual abilities under controlled laboratory conditions. She claimed not only to be able to move small objects—such as wineglasses, matchboxes, and compass needles—simply by concentrating on them, but also to influence biological systems, including healing wounds.

Kulagina reportedly demonstrated her healing abilities by holding her hands over injured or diseased areas, claiming to feel an intense energetic connection to the afflicted tissue. In multiple tests observed by Soviet parapsychologists, she was said to accelerate the healing of minor wounds and burns.

During episodes of psychokinesis, Kulagina described experiencing a series of physical symptoms. She would often feel a sharp pain in the back of her neck, suffer from blurred vision, and undergo a sudden and measurable rise in blood pressure.

These physiological effects were documented by medical personnel during experimental sessions, suggesting that whatever the mechanism behind her abilities, it placed considerable strain on her body. In some tests, her heartbeat reportedly accelerated to dangerous levels, and she was advised to stop practicing psychokinesis for health reasons.

Photographs and video footage taken during her demonstrations show objects moving across tables, seemingly without any physical contact. In one well-known experiment, she appeared to stop a frog's heart using only the power of her mind— though this particular claim has been hotly debated and criticized by sceptics.

Parapsychologist J. B. Rhine and others in the West cited Kulagina as one of the strongest cases supporting the possibility of psychokinesis.

Did Geller and Kulagina successfully harness the power of the right brain to bend spoons, make objects appear, or even move?

However, Wilson also noted that this explanation could not fully account for the poltergeist phenomenon. Geller and Kulagina could not cause objects to fly around a room at will, make bite marks or scratches appear on someone's skin, or cause fires to break out. And what about cases where more than one person seemed to be the focus of a haunting? Was it too fantastic to consider that an outside force—a 'spirit'—was feeding off someone's psychic energy to manifest itself?

Wilson was reminded of a case in 19th-century Paris, where a particularly violent poltergeist in the Rue des Noyers smashed every window in a house and threw objects about, including items that had apparently materialised from nowhere. Hippolyte Léon Denizard Rivail, a renowned intellectual and educationist in Paris, investigated the case. Rivail had become fascinated by spiritualism, having a friend named Becquet whose two daughters appeared able to communicate with the spirit world. Rivail decided to ask the 'spirits' several questions using automatic writing. Rivail was intrigued by the replies he received. According to the 'spirits,' the universe is pervaded by a magnetic 'fluid.' If this fluid cannot flow freely through a human being, the result is illness. The spirits also explained that incorporeal intelligences pervade the universe. Humans are incarnate spirits that unite with a physical body. Each lifetime brings the spirit closer to perfection as it undergoes various trials. However, between reincarnations, these spirits are able to wander the earth. It was these discarnate spirits that were responsible for poltergeists.

Allan Kardec (Rivail).

Rivail published *The Spirits' Book* in 1857, using the name Allan Kardec. According to the spirits, this was a name Rivail had used in a previous life. The book later became the foundation of *Spiritism*, a reincarnationist and spiritualist movement now practised in 36 countries with over 13 million followers worldwide.

Despite Rivail's belief in the spirit world, he was known to be critical of trance mediums, as most of the spirits who spoke through them said nothing about reincarnation—a concept Rivail firmly believed in.

Rivail asked the spirits about the haunting in Paris. They clarified that a mischievous spirit was causing the disturbances. The 'control' (a spirit named Saint Louis) summoned the poltergeist. The entity was bad-tempered and asked, "Why do you call me? Do you want some stones thrown at you?" Rivail enquired whether anyone in the house had assisted in deceiving the inhabitants. The entity replied that it had an excellent 'instrument'—a maid who had no idea she was being used and was the most frightened of all those in the house.

When asked how the poltergeist could throw objects around, it replied, "I helped myself through the electric nature of the girl, joined to my own... thus we were able to transport the objects between us."

The poltergeist claimed to be the ghost of a rag-and-bone man who had died about 50 years earlier. He had been addicted to drinking, and people had made fun of him. Because of this, he decided to return and play tricks on people. However, he insisted that he did this for fun, not out of malice.

Wilson was fascinated by the case and noted that it seemed to match a class of spirit described in *The Spirits' Book* as "ignorant, mischievous, unreasonable, and addicted to mockery. They meddle with everything and reply to every question without paying attention to the truth."

Rivail also asked the spirits about 'demonic possession' and whether spirits could unconsciously influence people. The spirits replied that their influence was greater than people might suppose. Indeed, they could often influence a person's thoughts and actions. When asked about the nature of possession, a spirit replied: "A spirit does not enter into a body as you enter a house. He assimilates himself to an incarnate spirit who has the same defects and the same qualities as himself in order that they may act conjointly." However, it also emphasised that a spirit can never fully subjugate the person it is possessing. Domination of a person is brought about through the cooperation of the 'possessed,' either through their weakness or willingness to be dominated. Interestingly, the spirit clarified that many individuals who seem possessed are not. Some are simply cases of madness or epilepsy and require a doctor rather than an exorcist.

Rivail then asked if exorcism worked. The answer was: "No. When bad spirits see anyone trying to influence them by such means, they laugh."

The exploration of the split brain phenomenon opened a new chapter in understanding the mysteries behind poltergeists and psychic phenomena. Colin Wilson's insights into the dual nature of the human mind—where the rational left brain and the intuitive right brain sometimes seem to operate as two distinct entities—offered a compelling framework to explain some extraordinary claims of telekinesis and psychokinesis. Historical cases involving individuals like Uri Geller and Nina Kulagina suggested that untapped mental powers might indeed manifest physically, possibly linked to the right hemisphere's hidden potential.

Yet, as Wilson recognized, the poltergeist phenomenon resisted simple explanations grounded solely in psychology or brain science. However, the work of Hippolyte Léon Denizard Rivail and the movement he inspired provided a spiritualist interpretation, suggesting that discarnate spirits—imperfect and playful—could exploit the vulnerabilities of living individuals to produce haunting phenomena.

Chapter Eleven
Earth Energies and Place-Centred Poltergeists

Colin Wilson was also intrigued by a theory first proposed by Alfred Watkins, an English businessman and amateur archaeologist, who believed that the countryside was covered by "long straight tracks" passing through sacred sites such as stone circles, burial mounds, and churches. Watkins originally assumed these were ancient trade routes. However, later researchers like John Michell suggested that these lines—dubbed *ley lines*—might represent invisible currents of earth energy.

Curiously, a higher incidence of paranormal activity has been reported in the vicinity of these ley lines, particularly at their crossing points. Wilson noted that many allegedly haunted locations—such as Borley Rectory in Suffolk, Ardachie Lodge in Scotland, and the historic City of York—appear to lie at the intersection of these lines. Could this alignment be more than mere coincidence?

Another influential figure in the field, archaeologist T.C. Lethbridge, developed similar ideas in the 1950s. His interest in dowsing and the paranormal led him to believe that ghosts could be linked to specific environmental conditions—particularly water or rock formations. Lethbridge proposed that magnetic fields associated with these elements might be capable of "recording" intense emotional experiences and later "playing them back" under suitable conditions—much like the way a magnetic field 'imprints' the sounds on an iron-oxide tape.

Wilson noted that dowsers can detect water by using a rod that appears to react to some magnetic force. Wilson experimented with dowsing and claimed success using rods in Cornwall, reinforcing his belief that some form of geomagnetic energy could be at work.

This led him to ask: could poltergeists be tapping into ley lines or magnetic energies associated with water and rocks to manifest through the subconscious mind— perhaps via the right hemisphere of the brain? And are ghosts and poltergeists not so different after all, both seemingly reliant on energy to appear? This might explain the sudden chill people often report in haunted locations. Was the poltergeist drawing energy not only from a human focus but also from the earth itself?

This line of inquiry raised another compelling theory: are some poltergeists location-based rather than person-based? The evidence suggests this could be true.

Take Dagworth Hall in Suffolk, for example. The present building dates from the 15th century, though a manor house is recorded at the site in the *Domesday Book*. In the 13th century, the monk and chronicler Ralph of Coggeshall described a peculiar haunting there in his *Chronicon Anglicanum*. The account features what we would now classify as a poltergeist:

"In the time of King Richard [1189-99], there appeared frequently, and for a long space of time, in the house of Sir Osberni de Bradewelle, at Daghewurthe in Suffolk, a certain fantastical spirit who conversed with the family of the aforesaid knight, always imitating the voice of a one-year old child. He called himself Malekin, and he said that his mother and brother dwelt in a neighbouring house, and that they often chided him because he left them and went to speak with people.

"The things which he did and said were both wonderful and very funny, and he often told people's secrets. At first the family of the knight were extremely terrified, but by degrees they became used to his words and silly actions, and conversed familiarly with him. He sometimes spoke English, in the dialect of the region, and sometimes in Latin, and he discussed the Scriptures with the chaplain of that same knight, just as he truly testified to us.

"He could be heard and felt too, but not seen, except once as a very small child clothed in a white tunic, in the chamber of a certain maiden. She had asked him to show himself to her, but he would not agree to this request until she swore by God that she would not touch or hold him. He also stated that he was born at Lavenham and that his mother had left him in part of a field where she was harvesting and that he had been taken away. He said that he had been in his present position seven years, and that after another seven years he should be restored to his former state of living with people. He said that he and the others had a sort of hat that made him invisible. He often asked for food and drink, which, when placed on a certain chest, immediately disappeared."

Given that Ralph of Coggeshall died around 1227, this account was written within living memory of the events.

Remarkably, a similar incident occurred centuries later. In the spring of 2000, Alan Murdie—Chairman of the Ghost Club and an authority on the paranormal—received a letter from Major Patrick de Vere Patey, a descendant of the Dagworth estate, about ghostly experiences within his family. He also mentioned Dagworth Hall.

"One other curious event in Dagworth was that in the 'Sixties,' a school inspector moved into the old part of the former Dagworth Hall only to leave pretty sharply due to what must have been the action of a Poltergeist behaving in the traditional manner."

Two incidents, separated by over 700 years, at the same location. As Murdie remarked, "That such a small hamlet should have two poltergeist-like incidents occurring at precisely the same spot so many centuries apart is certainly most intriguing."

Alan Gauld and Tony Cornell, in their 1979 study *Poltergeist*, examined 500 historical cases and concluded that roughly 24% were *place-centred*. In these cases, hauntings continued for over a year and frequently resumed after a gap—even when the original occupants had moved on.

Another example of a possible place-centered poltergeist comes from September 1966, when John Lennon, Ringo Starr, and their wives, Cynthia and Maureen, stayed in a villa in Almería, Spain. Lennon was filming *How I Won the War*, and the group took residence in a former convent. Soon after their arrival, strange things began to occur: objects vanished and reappeared in other rooms, lights flickered, and a persistent sense of an unseen presence haunted the villa.

One morning, Maureen found the laces on her nightgown tied in knots, though she had tied them in bows the previous night. During a party, the electricity failed, and a storm struck. As candles were lit, someone began singing. The others joined in— until, inexplicably, a beautiful, ethereal choral sound filled the room. Cynthia later recalled the moment as if *something* had taken control of their voices. The otherworldly choir sang with them for half an hour. The spell only broke when the lights came back on.

Another potential case of a place-centred poltergeist is the Seven Stars Pub in Robertsbridge, Sussex. Paranormal investigator Andrew Green recorded that the pub had seen twelve different licensees between 1971 and 2003. Every one of them— and their families and staff—reported poltergeist-like disturbances.

The evidence explored in this chapter suggests that poltergeists may not always be tied solely to individuals but can also be linked to specific locations. From ancient halls like Dagworth to modern villas and public houses, recurring disturbances across centuries point to the possibility of place-centred energies at work. Whether through earth energies, magnetic fields, or residual emotional imprints, these mysterious forces seem capable of interacting with the human mind—and perhaps the environment itself. For Wilson and others, such cases hint at a deeper, largely untapped layer of reality where consciousness, geology, and the paranormal may intersect.

Chapter Twelve
Poltergeists and Possessed Relics

While poltergeist phenomena are usually associated with individuals, numerous cases suggest that certain objects can also serve as focal points for such disturbances. In some of the most enduring and unsettling accounts, human skulls appear to act as conduits or anchors for supernatural activity. One of the most intriguing examples comes from Lancashire, England, and concerns Timberbottom Farm. In 1751, two human skulls—one female, one male—were discovered in Bradshaw Brook. One of them bore a distinct wound on the left side, as if it had been struck with an axe. Initially, the skulls were placed on the mantelpiece at Timberbottom Farm, a nearby building in Bradshaw. Soon after, unexplained and increasingly violent activity plagued the household. Pots and pans were thrown across the kitchen, strange bangs echoed through the house, and the sounds of fighting were frequently heard.

In one particularly chilling incident, the farmer and his wife claimed to have returned home and opened the kitchen door to see two men, dressed in antiquated clothing, engaged in violent combat. A young woman's ghost was said to be watching the fight in silent horror. This ghostly confrontation reportedly repeated every month, like a tragic scene trapped in an endless loop.

In an attempt to stop the disturbances, the skulls were removed and buried in the churchyard of nearby Bradshaw Chapel. However, the haunting only intensified. Loud noises and knocking were reported after each burial attempt. The skulls were unearthed and returned to the farm more than once, and any attempt to dispose of them—such as throwing them back into the brook—was met with immediate, dramatic disturbances.

Over the years, several theories emerged about the origin of the skulls. One tale claimed they belonged to two robbers who were killed by a servant while attempting to break into the farm in 1680. Another suggested the skulls were those of a couple—a farmer who killed his wife before taking his own life. A third story told of a servant who fell in love with a daughter of the wealthy Bradshaw family. After the servant was killed by the woman's brother, the young woman died of grief. The skulls, it was said, were reunited in death so their spirits could remain together.

Colonel Henry M. Hardcastle, owner of nearby Bradshaw Hall, acquired the skulls in the early 20th century. When he placed them on the family Bible, the disturbances at Timberbottom Farm—now dubbed "Skull House"—ceased. But the pattern of activity would return whenever the skulls were moved or separated.

In 1995, Mr. Arthur Clifford of Bolton wrote to *The Bolton News* after the paper published an article about the skulls. In his letter, he recounted the story of the local milkman, James Heywood of Timberbottom Farm. In 1922, when Arthur was just eight years old, he remembered Mrs. Heywood delivering milk and telling his mother that the family's cat and dog had run off. The previous night, Mrs. Heywood had heard knocking and scratching at the door. Assuming someone had returned the missing animals, she opened it—only to find no one there. Instead, she heard footsteps pass her, cross the room, and ascend the stairs. It was later discovered that this strange event coincided with Colonel Hardcastle sending one of the skulls away to be remounted.

In 1927, one of the skulls was found to be disintegrating. It was taken to Manchester for repairs. During its absence, the farm was again troubled at night by bangs, footsteps, and knocks.

In 1939, the Bolton Journal and Guardian reported that the ghost had "risen to activity again."

The newspaper reported that the Heywood family had been disturbed on the night of Friday, October 20. Just before 11 p.m., while in bed, they were awakened by loud noises coming from downstairs. Doors were heard opening and closing repeatedly. The sounds were so loud it seemed as though someone was lifting the doors off their hinges. Drawers were heard being pulled out and slammed shut. Then came heavy footsteps on the stairs. After a pause, the steps descended again, and the rooms below shook with raps and bangs. The footsteps returned to the stairs and once again retreated.

The noises continued for nearly two hours before John Heywood and his lodger, Tom Lomas, armed themselves with cudgels and searched the house. As they reached the bottom of the stairs, they heard the latch of the front door lift and footsteps cross the flagstones outside. However, they found nothing out of place. Even the family cat was calmly warming itself by the fire. They returned to bed, only to find that the disturbances had resumed. The footsteps went up and down the stairs several more times—described as sounding like "a heavy-built man, wearing big boots." Mrs. Heywood said the ghost paused halfway up the stairs for ten minutes during its final ascent and believed it had entered a small bedroom.

The disturbances did not stop until 4 a.m. Mr. and Mrs. Lomas left the farm shortly afterward, saying they were too frightened to stay. Mr. and Mrs. Heywood declined to move, having grown used to the sounds over the years. However, Mr. Heywood noted that the noises this time were louder and more prolonged than ever before.

He believed the ghost would remain even after the farmhouse was demolished, as it had recently been declared unfit for human habitation. Some speculated that the skulls were protesting the proposed destruction of the farm, though others noted that one of the skulls had again been temporarily removed from the Bible for repairs at the time.

Colonel Hardcastle, after reading Harry Price's book on the haunting of Borley Rectory, decided to write to him. In a series of letters exchanged in November 1940, the colonel shared several intriguing details about the farm, which had been in his family for generations. According to him, the poltergeist had plagued the property for approximately 150 years. In addition to earlier disturbances, the entity reportedly had a peculiar habit of opening and closing a specific chest of drawers in a room above the kitchen—a place also known for frequent tapping sounds. At times, the household cat would follow the taps as they moved about the room.

These visitations occurred at long intervals—once after a gap of nine years, and on another occasion, eleven.

Colonel Hardcastle also recounted a notable incident involving the skulls. During a particularly intense period of activity many years earlier, his grandfather had them buried in the local churchyard in an attempt to end the disturbances. However, as with the other attempts to bury them, this led to a violent outbreak of manifestations. The skulls were subsequently exhumed and placed on the family Bible, where they remained. The woman's skull was eventually mounted in silver and set on a stand.

Roughly nine years before his 1940 correspondence, Colonel Hardcastle had accidentally damaged the silver mounting and sent the skull to a Manchester silversmith for repairs. That very day, violent disturbances erupted at the farm and continued until the skull was returned to its place beside its male counterpart on the Bible.

Harry Price promised to investigate the case personally but was prevented from doing so by the Second World War. However, he did mention the case in his 1945 book, *Poltergeist Over England: Three Centuries of Mischievous Ghosts*.

Turton Tower, a manor house dating back to the 1400s, received the skulls in 1948—the year of Price's death. The building became a museum, and the skulls were displayed in a glass case. In 1964, a Manchester student interested in the occult asked Turton Council for permission to examine the skulls and "call the ghost out of retirement." The request was discussed by the Finance and General Purposes Committee but ultimately rejected. The council clerk, Mr. H. Lewis, commented tersely: "I don't believe in this twaddle, but assuming that people do believe it, I don't think we should risk terrifying the people who live in the houses on the site [of the farm]." The chairman of the Finance Committee was less sceptical, saying he believed "it wrong to mess about with such things."

Today, the skulls remain locked away in a private room at Turton Tower, still resting on a Bible, and still considered too dangerous—or too sacred—to be disturbed.

Unlike more conventional poltergeist cases, where a person is believed to be the catalyst, the Timberbottom haunting suggests that some disturbances can be object-based. The phenomenon was clearly tied to the presence, placement, or separation of the skulls. When the skulls were removed, activity flared up. When they were kept together, particularly when placed atop a family Bible, the disturbances ceased.

Throughout history, skulls have often been viewed as powerful symbols—both in life and death. In some cultures, skulls were believed to hold the soul or essence of a person, making them potent objects in rituals or hauntings. The idea that skulls can act as vessels for spirits has been a recurring theme in folklore and occultism around the world, reinforcing the notion that these remains carry energy or consciousness beyond physical death.

Another interesting case involving a supposedly haunted object dates from 1937. However, in this instance, the apparent source of the haunting was not a skull, but a wardrobe!

The *Morning Post* for Thursday, August 19, 1937, featured an unusually intriguing advertisement tucked away in its personal column. It read:

> **FOR SALE** – Haunted wardrobe. Advertiser will be glad to deliver to anybody interested, complete with ghost, which would also no doubt feel more at home if welcomed. – Write Mrs. Barclay, Carterton Manor, Oxon.

This peculiar notice sparked immediate public interest, but the bizarre series of events that led Mrs. Barclay to place such an advertisement had begun three years earlier, in 1934.

At the time, Mrs. Barclay had attended the sale of personal effects at a country house near Streatley in Berkshire. Among the many items for auction, her attention was drawn to a large Victorian wardrobe crafted from rich walnut. The piece stood an imposing seven feet tall and measured seven feet six inches across. It featured four drawers, mirrors, and an undeniable sense of grandeur. Struck by its stately presence and fine craftsmanship, Mrs. Barclay purchased the wardrobe for £10 and arranged for it to be delivered to her residence, Carterton Manor in Oxfordshire.

Once it arrived, she placed the wardrobe in the guest bedroom, where it stood undisturbed for nearly two years. For a time, it appeared to be no more than a handsome, if slightly oversized, piece of Victorian furniture.

However, in the spring of 1937, strange occurrences began to trouble the peace of Carterton Manor. Mrs. Barclay and her household staff started to hear unexplained rattling and banging noises emanating from the guest room. Friends who came to stay soon began to ask—some with amusement, others with concern—if there was anything unusual about the wardrobe. Several visitors claimed the doors had opened and closed entirely on their own.

As the disturbances persisted and increased in intensity, Mrs. Barclay became more alarmed. One evening, she and her secretary, Mr. East, resolved to investigate the matter more thoroughly. As they approached the wardrobe, an astonishing thing happened: the center door suddenly flew open with such force that it shattered the mirror on another door. Shaken and alarmed, they quickly abandoned their search, unable to make sense of what they had just witnessed.

But this was only the beginning.

Not long after, Mrs. Barclay saw a figure emerging from the wardrobe. She described it as a bent, wizened old man, dressed in antiquated clothing and wearing a deerstalker hat. The ghostly figure silently walked down the stairs and exited through the front door. The apparition reappeared on another night. On that occasion, she bravely attempted to touch it, but as her hand reached out, the figure vanished before her eyes.

The ghost continued to make appearances, each time following the same peculiar routine: stepping out of the wardrobe, descending the stairs, and leaving through the front entrance. The spectral visitor was seen on multiple occasions, not only by Mrs. Barclay but also by her brother and Mr. East. On one particularly unsettling evening, the figure stared directly at Mrs. Barclay for a full minute as she once again attempted to approach it. Then, as before, it turned and left the house, slamming the door behind it with a loud bang.

The ghostly manifestations soon became more than mere curiosities; they became nuisances. In an interview, Mrs. Barclay complained, "I am not psychic, nor am I nervous, but this wretched ghost will make such a noise. He clatters across the landing and shuffles down the stairs, and the noise is often exasperatingly loud."

As word of the haunting spread, friends and acquaintances became reluctant to visit Carterton Manor, let alone stay overnight. One particularly sceptical friend, Mr. E. Rundle—the landlord of the Plough Inn in Clanfield—attempted to tie the wardrobe shut with string, believing the disturbances to be some sort of prank. But by morning, the string was inexplicably lying on the floor, the doors wide open.

Matters continued to deteriorate. Mrs. Barclay, unable to sleep due to the noise, moved her bed to a different part of the house. More disturbingly, the ghost appeared to take a particular dislike to the household staff. On one occasion, it reportedly kicked the butler in the shins. The butler promptly resigned, followed soon after by the maid. Even the cook, perhaps the most stoic of the staff, decided to leave.

Faced with a dwindling household and an increasingly distressed reputation, Mrs. Barclay decided drastic action was necessary. Thus, the now-famous advertisement was placed in *The Morning Post*.

The response was overwhelming. Curious thrill-seekers, spiritualists, sceptics, and journalists alike flooded her with letters and telegrams. Several individuals even traveled to Carterton Manor in hopes of seeing the ghost—or at least acquiring the haunted wardrobe. One telegram from Chobham in Surrey cheekily asked if she could guarantee the ghost's presence. Mrs. Barclay laughed at the absurdity, but as she sat down to lunch shortly afterward, the ghost appeared once more—this time standing silently in front of the mantelpiece before vanishing again.

With media attention growing, Mrs. Barclay and Mr. East allowed two newspaper reporters to spend the night in the house and conduct a vigil. For the first hour, all was quiet. Then, a soft rustling noise began to emanate from the wardrobe—reportedly like berries falling from trees. The sound intensified. A button was found lying on the floor, directly in front of the wardrobe. Everyone present swore it had not been there before. At that moment, Mrs. Barclay cried out, "He is here!" though no one else could see anything unusual.

She claimed the ghost had entered the room and then walked out, unseen by all but her.

The vigil ended in farce. A practical joker, dressed in white, had infiltrated the garden, shouting and trying to frighten the group. Mr. East gave chase and drove the intruder off the premises. It was decided to move the wardrobe outside, placing it in the garden to reduce the disturbance inside the house.

Even as the wardrobe sat exposed to the elements, offers continued to pour in. One would-be buyer proposed marriage to Mrs. Barclay, while another asked if the ghost would be happy in a small suburban home.

Ultimately, Mrs. Barclay accepted a £50 offer—five times what she had originally paid—from her friend Mr. Rundle. He moved it to the outhouse of his inn in Clanfield, noting with some bravado that he didn't believe in ghosts and intended to keep the wardrobe in his own bedroom.

Word quickly spread that the infamous wardrobe had found a new home, and Clanfield became the next target for pranks. Local youths, donning white sheets or hurling bricks at the inn's roof, kept the village in a state of suspense and irritation. A second vigil was planned but was soon disrupted when a group of rowdy boys began wailing and throwing brickbats outside the property.

Despite his scepticism, Mr. Rundle experienced his own unsettling moment when one of the wardrobe doors began trembling violently on its own during the first night in the outhouse. His wife also reported strange noises—rattling and a sound reminiscent of an aeroplane's engine—coming from within the wardrobe.

Seeking rational explanations, Mr. Rundle moved the wardrobe into a spare room inside the inn and undertook a thorough search. He suspected the ghost might be tied to a hidden object or concealed compartment. Despite his efforts, he found no secret panels, compartments, or signs of a hidden past. A furniture expert who was later called in confirmed the wardrobe had undergone some alterations over the years, but found nothing of note.

After that final investigation, the wardrobe fell silent. No more noises, no more apparitions. The ghost, it seemed, had either found peace or simply moved on.

The haunting at Carterton Manor presents a compelling case that defies simple categorization. While initially resembling a traditional poltergeist case due to the physical disturbances associated with the wardrobe, the manifestation of a full-bodied apparition and the wardrobe's role as a focal point suggest elements of a residual haunting. The cessation of phenomena upon the wardrobe's disassembly further complicates the classification, indicating that the object itself might have been an anchor for the disturbances.

This case exemplifies the complexity of paranormal phenomena, where overlapping characteristics challenge conventional definitions. The Carterton Manor haunting underscores the necessity for a nuanced approach in investigating and understanding such occurrences.

The psychological impact of haunted objects often feeds into the phenomena, potentially intensifying experiences. The fear and anxiety generated by such objects can amplify perceptions of supernatural activity, blurring the lines between genuine paranormal occurrences and those shaped by human suggestion and belief.

From a scientific and parapsychological perspective, theories such as residual hauntings and psychometry attempt to explain how objects can hold or channel energy. Residual hauntings suggest that traumatic or emotionally charged events can imprint themselves on the environment or objects, creating a replay of the original event. Psychometry involves the idea that sensitive individuals can "read" the history or emotions attached to an object by touching it, implying that objects can store and transmit psychic energy.

This raises the question: does this "emotional imprint" or residual energy attract the attention of a poltergeist or other spiritual entity? Could poltergeists themselves be drawn to, or even born from, this trapped energy? The Timberbottom and Carterton Manor cases suggests a complex relationship between spirit, energy, and physical objects—one that blurs the boundaries between haunting and possession, between the living and the dead.

Chapter Thirteen

The Black Monk of Pontefract

Colin Wilson personally investigated a poltergeist case in Pontefract. Indeed, it would become the basis for his book on the poltergeist phenomenon—*Poltergeist!* An amateur historian had contacted him about a council house in the Yorkshire town. Jean and Joe Pritchard, along with their two children, Philip and Diane, had moved into the house at 30 East Drive in 1966.

The house stood on a post-World War II council estate. Unbeknownst to the Pritchards, the previous occupants, Bill and Barbara Farrar, had experienced strange activity in the house. Objects had moved, voices were heard in empty rooms, and rips and tears appeared on a settee and the hood of a toy pram. Jane, their two-year-old daughter, was found with scratches and blood marks on her face. Assuming she had done this herself, her parents put cotton mittens on her hands. Despite this, marks continued to appear. The family decided to move out because Mrs. Farrar could not bear to live there any longer.

It was not long after the Pritchards moved in that strange things began to happen. At first, in the lounge, a grey-white powder, like chalk dust, suddenly appeared floating in midair. Then, neat little puddles of water appeared on the kitchen floor. A plant, minus its pot, was found on the stairs; the crockery cupboard would shake, and the rooms would become icy cold. Lights would go on and off, and knocks would sound throughout the house, followed by the window frames rattling. The most alarming incident was the discovery of a wedding photograph of Jean and Joe Pritchard. It had been slashed from end to end, as if by a knife.

At first, the activity appeared to be centred on 15-year-old Phillip Pritchard, but this was abruptly transferred to his sister Diane (then aged 14) during the second period of assault, which started suddenly after two years of peace and lasted from late 1968 to mid-1969. The icy chill returned, and objects would fly about the house. Once, a wallpaper roll was seen to stand on its end and sway like a snake. This was followed by a carpet sweeper that flew into the air and started to swing about as if being used as a weapon. Paint brushes flew about, and a wooden pelmet was seen tearing itself out of a wall in Diane's bedroom. It then hurled itself through the window.

The family nicknamed the poltergeist "Mr. Nobody" (Jean Pritchard later named it "Fred"), an entity that reserved its main activity for when the family went to bed. The family heard loud bangs akin to someone beating a drum, and ornaments began to levitate and fly across the room. The lights would go out, and when the mains switch under the stairs was checked, it was found turned off. Tape was placed over the 'on' switch, but it made no difference. The lights went out again, and the tape had vanished. It was decided to hold an exorcism, and a local vicar, the Reverend Davy, agreed to visit the house one Thursday evening to discuss the matter. The poltergeist remained silent during his visit, but as he was about to leave, there were two loud thumps, followed by a small brass candlestick leaping off the mantelpiece onto the floor. Davy blamed the incident on subsidence, but he was then treated to the sight of another candlestick rising from the shelf and floating in front of his face. A loud crash sounded from the lounge next door. Rushing into the room, they found every piece of china from a cupboard scattered across the floor. However, not a single item was smashed or damaged. Davy no longer dismissed the family's concerns. He thought there was something evil in the house and suggested they move.

The poltergeist continued to plague the family. That same night, Diane saw a huge shadow appear on a wall. An oak hall stand, with an electric sewing machine resting on it, then levitated and moved towards her. The stand fell onto her. Fortunately, it was not pressing down on her with all its weight. At first, Jean and Phillip Pritchard tried to move it off her without success. Jean then advised Diane to lie still and relax. She did so and felt a sudden change in the force holding her down. Her parents then managed to free her. A group of local councillors visited the house, triggering another instance of violence. Before leaving, the mayor expressed surprise that the family's grandmother clock was still intact. A half-hour later, something threw the clock down the stairs and smashed it to pieces.

Diane was taken to bed by her mother. The moment the girl switched off the light, something pulled off the bedclothes, and the room turned icy cold. She had a strong sense that there was a presence in the room, and then her mattress shot into the air, and she found herself on the floor with it on top of her. This happened another four times.

The haunting attracted local press attention, and people began to refer to 30 East Drive as the "haunted house." Jean Pritchard invited an acquaintance named Rene Holden—who had a reputation for being "a bit psychic"—to visit the house. Nothing happened on her first visit, so she decided to return the following week. This time, she witnessed lights going out, a sudden blast of wind, and the sound of objects flying around the room. She also heard a tapping sound on a window. When the lights came back on, they discovered a partially eaten sandwich bearing huge teeth marks. Mrs. Holden asked to keep the sandwich as proof. She wrapped it up, but it disintegrated into crumbs within a few days.

Mrs. Holden returned to the house the following weekend and witnessed further phenomena, including objects being thrown downstairs and the sensation that her hair was swarming with tiny creatures. She became convinced that the poltergeist was drawing energy from the solar plexus of the children and suggested that it was also taking energy from an underground stream beneath the property. It is interesting to note that a large stone well, believed to be medieval, also lay beneath the house.

Joe Pritchard's sister, Maude Peerce, also visited and witnessed the poltergeist at work. The lights went out, the refrigerator door swung open, and a milk jug floated out. It moved toward Maude and hovered above her head, then tilted and poured the milk over her. Maude blamed the children, but Jean pointed out that they were nowhere near her. Deciding to spend the night in the same room as Jean, the pair were shocked to see Maude's fur gloves appear simultaneously at the top and bottom of the door. Throwing a boot at them, Maude shouted, "Get away. You're evil!" The gloves vanished—only to reappear, floating into the room. One of them appeared to beckon to them. When they declined to follow, the glove clenched into a fist and shook threateningly at Maude. She responded by singing "Onward, Christian Soldiers." The gloves, apparently enjoying the performance, began to conduct the singing. Taking no chances, Maude took the gloves into the garden and burned them.

The poltergeist activity continued. Eggs would explode, filling the room with a pleasant scent. Door handles were smeared with jam and festooned with toilet paper. A local Catholic attempted to exorcise the house using holy water, but it made no difference. Water was seen running down the walls, and that same night, the house was filled with the sound of drumming, while the furniture was overturned. The poltergeist appeared to resent the exorcism. A crucifix was thrown at Diane, and inverted gold crosses were found painted on doors. The precision of the painting suggested that a stencil had been used. However, attempts to replicate the effect failed; the glossy surface of the doors caused the paint to run into globules.

Neighbours reported seeing a dim glow around the house, and on one occasion, Jean witnessed a shower of keys falling down the chimney. The poltergeist had apparently gathered all the keys in the house and thrown them down the flue, including one old-looking key that Jean could not identify.

An apparition of a tall, hooded figure was also seen. Mrs. May Mountain, a neighbour, reported seeing it in her own home. She described the figure as tall, dressed in a black monk's habit, with a cowl over its face. She felt no fear—only curiosity—before the figure vanished.

However, 30 East Drive remained the focal point for most of the activity. The drumming intensified, and the sounds of a farmyard—including a cow and chickens—were heard from a bedroom. Breathing was heard outside bedroom doors at night. On one occasion, Mrs. Holden felt a hand touch her on the back of the head after the lights went out, then saw the lower half of  the monk as she crossed the lounge. Diane was once pulled upstairs, leaving red finger marks on her throat.

Large footprints were found on the wet hallway carpet one morning, and both Diane and Phillip saw a figure through a frosted glass door. When Phillip opened the door, he saw a monk disappearing into the kitchen floor.

A friend, newly returned from Scotland, suggested hanging garlic over the doors to ward off the spirits. The family followed his advice—and the manifestations ceased.

A local man, Tom Cunniff, researched the case and discovered that a priory had once stood in the area. There was also a legend of a Cluniac monk who had been hanged for raping a girl during the reign of Henry VIII. The gallows had reportedly stood on the hill above where the Pritchards' house was built, and a bridge named "Priest's Bridge" had once stood on the site. Could the ghost of the monk be responsible?

Colin Wilson decided to investigate and found no evidence to support the story of a monk executed for rape. However, he did discover that during the English Civil War, a local priest had been executed after being accused of spying for the Royalists. The area had seen clashes between the armies of Parliament and King Charles I. There was also a rich tradition of ghostly sightings in the region. Despite the lack of historical evidence for the executed monk, Wilson interviewed the Pritchards and was convinced by their sincerity.

Clearly, something had haunted the house— for others had also witnessed the phenomena.

The Pritchard family continued living at 30 East Drive. Eventually, Diane and Phillip moved out. Joe Pritchard died in 1986, and Jean continued to live at the property for another 25 years. People still claim the house is haunted. Bil Bungay, a film producer and author, later bought the property and began charging for overnight stays. The team from *Most Haunted* filmed an episode at the house and claimed to have experienced paranormal activity there. Online commentators later accused *Most Haunted* of cheating—a claim the team has consistently denied. Since then, many others who have stayed overnight at 30 East Drive have reported ghostly activity.

The haunting of 30 East Drive remains one of the most compelling and perplexing cases in the study of paranormal phenomena. Whether one views it through the lens of supernatural belief, psychological theory, or environmental influence, the consistency and intensity of the events reported by multiple witnesses over decades cannot be easily dismissed.

Despite attempts at exorcism, scientific investigation, and historical research, the source of the terror remains elusive. While theories have ranged from the restless spirit of a medieval monk to manifestations powered by underground energy or emotional trauma, no single explanation has proven definitive. What is clear, however, is that something unusual occurred—and perhaps continues to occur—at this otherwise ordinary house in Pontefract.

Chapter Fourteen

The Bell Witch

Does the Pontefract case demonstrate that the right brain's psychic energy is not the only cause of poltergeists? As we've already discussed, are some cases object or location-based, involving the presence of a spirit? In 1972, Ian Stevenson wrote an article in the *Journal of the American SPR* titled *Poltergeists: Are they living or are they dead?* In it, he argued there are two types of poltergeist disturbances: one linked to the unconscious mind, and another suggesting the presence of an entity or spirit.

According to Kardec in *The Spirits' Book*, spirits aim to evolve but may choose their own paths. This observation struck Colin Wilson, who often noted how immature poltergeists behaved like spoiled children—swearing, claiming to be the devil, and making scandalous allegations.

Wilson wondered if poltergeists were spirits lacking purpose, acting like bored humans. Was their misbehaviour merely a tactic to attract attention, and once successful, would they improve their behaviour or relocate to another location?

However, as seen, not all poltergeists are harmless pranksters. They can turn violent and even cause serious physical harm. One recorded case involved a death, with the poltergeist claiming responsibility.

The Bell Home.

In 1817, John Bell, a farmer in Robertson County, Tennessee, lived with his wife Lucy and nine children. One day, Bell saw an apparition resembling a dog with a rabbit's head in a cornfield. He fired his gun, but it vanished. Around the same time, his daughter Betsy saw the apparition of girl in a green dress swinging from a tree; his son Drew saw an enormous unknown bird that flew off as he approached it; and a family slave spotted a snarling black dog, which vanished when threatened with a stick.

After the cornfield incident, strange beating sounds began outside the Bell home, growing louder nightly. Soon, noises appeared inside—scratches, knocks, wing beats, and sounds like dogs fighting. Then came the poltergeist's physical disturbances: pulling clothes and pillows off beds, overturning chairs and throwing stones. Most frightening of all, choking and gasping sounds likened to someone being strangled were also heard in the house.

Betsy seemed the focus; disturbances occurred only when she was present. The haunting worsened—walls shook, and Richard Williams Bell woke to his hair being pulled so hard he feared the top of his head would be pulled off. Betsy, in a room above, also screamed that something had been pulling her hair.

Betsy Bell.

The family asked a neighbour, James Johnston, for advice. He visited the house and heard the ghost make a sound likened to someone sucking air through their teeth. He told it to be quiet, and the noise suddenly stopped. However, it has been noted by Colin Wilson and others that poltergeists often dislike being told what to do and appear to react more favourably if treated in a friendly manner. Ordering them about can make the problem worse. Whatever the case, Betsy became the target of the poltergeist, pulling her hair or slapping her face until it went red.

The poltergeist began producing human-like sounds—at first whispers and gasps. Betsy grew tired and fainted; observers noted her voice stopped when unconscious, leading some to suspect she faked the noises. John Bell suffered too; his tongue swelled, his jaw stiffened as if stuck with a stick, making eating impossible. The poltergeist boasted it would torment him until death.

Betsy was sent away, but the poltergeist followed, speaking softly: "Betsy, you should not have come over here; you know I can follow you anywhere. Now get a good night's sleep." A gentle hand patted her cheek, and the voice reassured her that she wouldn't experience any further disturbances that night.

During Betsy's absence, the Bell home was quiet. When she returned, so did the poltergeist. A friend, Frank Miles, promised to protect Betsy from further abuse by the 'Spirit,' but his promises were mocked by the poltergeist, who responded, "You go home; you can do no good here." It then attacked Betsy, slapping her and pulling her hair before turning on Miles and knocking him over.

The poltergeist delighted in tormenting visitors—slapping them, pulling off bedclothes, and throwing stones and pieces of wood at the children. If the children threw stones back, the spirit returned them immediately. However, the children were never harmed when it did so.

It identified as 'Old Kate Batts witch.' Kate Batts was a neighbour whose brother-in-law had a dispute with John Bell over the sale of a slave. Following this, the poltergeist became locally known as the 'Bell Witch.'

Four additional voices claimed to be members of the witch's family: Blackdog, Mathematics, Cypocryphy, and Jerusalem. Jerusalem sounded like a boy; Blackdog, harsh and masculine; the others delicate and feminine.

Though the witch hated John Bell, it was kinder to the family, especially Lucy, calling her the "most perfect woman living." When Lucy fell ill, the witch lamented, "Luce, poor Luce," and showered her with hazelnuts. At Betsy's birthday, it materialized a basket of fruit "from the West Indies."

A 'witch doctor' administered medicine to Betsy, which made her vomit pins and needles, amusing the witch, who, laughing, declared Betsy could open a shop if she fell ill again.

On another occasion, the witch pulled a sledge around the house three times while telling the children sitting on it to "Hold tight." It whispered to Betsy the location of hidden gold, leading to a fruitless treasure hunt. The witch laughed and teased the family about their failure to find it.

The poltergeist disliked a Black slave, Anky, once covering her with a white spittle-like substance. Jealous of Betsy's engagement to Joshua Gardner, it whispered, "Please, Betsy Bell, don't have Joshua Gardner." Betsy ended the relationship.

However, the Bell Witch continued to reserve its real venom for John Bell. It would pull off his shoes and curse him when he was lying sick in bed. Once, the witch struck him in the face so hard that he had to sit down. The witch would sing songs and laugh maniacally as John Bell's face and body jerked and twitched. It had now been persecuting John Bell for some three years. Finally, taking to his bed, he fell into a stupor. In the medicine cupboard, his son, John Jr., found a bottle containing a smokey-looking liquid. The witch was heard to call out, "It's useless for you to try to relieve old Jack; I've got him this time." Asked about the bottle, it replied, "I put it there and gave old Jack a dose last night while he was asleep, which fixed him."

A doctor was summoned, and the liquid was tested on a cat, which jumped and whirled around before falling down dead. John Bell died the next day; the witch shrieked in triumph and sang, "Row me up some brandy, O."

Following John Bell's death, the witch appeared to lose interest in haunting the family. John Jr. asked it to allow him to speak to his deceased father, but it refused, stating that one could not bring the dead back. However, it did tell John to go to a window on a cold day where he saw footprints suddenly appear in the snow, the witch claiming that these were his father's footsteps. John did not bother to check if they matched his father's boots.

In 1821, some four years after the Bell Witch had first made itself known, the family was having supper when they heard a loud noise in the chimney. Suddenly, something that resembled a cannonball rolled into the room and exploded in a cloud of smoke. A voice then called out, "I'm going and will be gone for seven years - goodbye to all."

Seven years later, the witch returned, pulling bedcovers and making noises. By then, only Lucy and the two youngest children remained; others, including Betsy, had left. Ignored, the witch's disturbances ceased after two weeks. As poltergeists seemingly thrive on attention, its sudden departure is hardly surprising. John Jr. later claimed that the witch had said it would return to one of his descendants in 107 years. The witch did not fulfil its promise; no member of the Bell family reported the witch's return in 1935.

Nandor Fodor, in *The Story of the Poltergeist Down the Centuries*, suggested poltergeists are sexual in origin and theorized the Bell Witch stemmed from an incestuous attack on Betsy by her father, with hatred manifesting as 'recurrent spontaneous psychokinesis.' Colin Wilson disagreed. Poltergeists usually take delight in embarrassing people by revealing their intimate secrets. For example, it had no qualms about revealing details about Betsy's relationship with Joshua. So why had it remained silent on this matter if Betsy's father had tried or committed incest with his daughter? And what of the fact that Betsy had also been subjected to aggression from the poltergeist? And how was the witch able to return to the household after Betsy left home and married?

Fodor noted the witch's denial of the dead returning proved it was not a spirit of a dead person. But poltergeists are rarely truthful. He concluded the poltergeist was "a fragment of a living personality that has broken free in some mysterious way from the three-dimensional limitations of the mind of the main personality."

If true, it remains unclear how the energy of a fragmented personality can, for instance, produce apparitions or cause the teleportation of objects.

Sigmund Freud's concept of the power of the unconscious mind is no longer widely accepted, casting doubt on the long-standing theory held by some parapsychologists that this alone explains all poltergeist activity. Perhaps, as Allan Kardec suggested in *The Spirits' Book*, the truth lies elsewhere: that some poltergeists are indeed spirits of the dead, while others may be 'elementals'—

lower forms of intelligence that exist, for reasons unknown, to disrupt and unsettle the living.

Colin Wilson saw the Bell Witch as a classic example of this theory. The Bell family's many children and rural poverty likely created tensions attracting mischievous entities. The witch did claim to be multiple spirits—unless it lied.

At the haunting's start, John Bell fired at a dog-like creature in a field. Poltergeists dislike aggression and often react violently to it. Was this creature a manifestation of the witch? Did Bell's aggression fuel its hatred for him?

The Bell Witch haunting remains one of the most compelling and perplexing poltergeist cases in American history, challenging simple explanations. It straddles the line between spiritual manifestation and psychological phenomena, leaving open questions about the true nature of such disturbances. Whether the Bell Witch was a restless spirit, a mischievous elemental, or a projection of human psychic energy, the case illustrates the complexity and diversity of poltergeist activity.

In popular culture, the term *poltergeist* is often used interchangeably with *ghost*, but researchers and paranormal theorists have long argued that there are significant differences between the two.

In truth, the line between ghosts and poltergeists is often blurred. Some cases begin as a classic haunting—with footsteps and ghostly sightings—before escalating into violent, poltergeist-like behaviour. Others seem purely energetic, yet develop intelligent characteristics. This has led some researchers to suggest that these are not separate categories, but points on a spectrum.

At one end lie residual hauntings—replays of the past, without consciousness. In the middle, poltergeists—energetic, perhaps unconscious, occasionally intelligent. At the far end, spirits or ghosts—entities with awareness, intention, and memory.

To better understand how poltergeists and ghosts differ—and where they may overlap—we may turn to two case studies from the annals of psychical research and spiritualist history.

The Ghost: The Woman in Black (1882)
Type: Intelligent haunting

This case, investigated by members of the Society for Psychical Research (SPR), involved a recurring veiled female apparition seen by multiple members of a family in Cheltenham. Witnesses described a distinct personality: she was melancholy, calm, and seemed tethered to a particular space and action.

In 1882, Captain F.W. Despard leased a house in Cheltenham and renamed it *Donore*. Soon after moving in with his wife, children, and several servants, the family began experiencing strange phenomena, particularly involving a ghostly figure: a tall woman in black, often described as wearing a widow's outfit and holding a handkerchief to her face as if crying.

The first sighting occurred in June 1882 when Rosina Despard, aged 19, encountered the apparition outside her bedroom. Over the next few years, Rosina saw the figure more than a dozen times, often in the drawing-room or descending the stairs. Her siblings, including six-year-old Wilfred and sister Edith, also witnessed the ghost, as did servants, neighbours, and family friends. Reports included footsteps, swishing drapery, slamming doors, and the rattling of handles. Several claimed to see the figure appear solid and lifelike—yet it would vanish suddenly or elude physical contact.

Rosina attempted to communicate with the ghost and kept detailed written records of her encounters. The apparition appeared to show intelligence but never spoke. The Despards consulted the Society for Psychical Research (SPR), and investigator Frederic Myers documented the case extensively. He encouraged efforts to photograph the ghost and even conducted interviews with witnesses, including staff members who had suffered severe fright, one developing partial facial paralysis from fear.

The ghost was believed by some to be the second wife of a previous resident, Mrs. Swinhoe, who had died in the house. She was said to have hidden jewelry beneath the floorboards, which the Despards searched for without success. The haunting peaked between 1884–1886, then gradually faded. In later years, the apparition appeared less solid and eventually ceased entirely by 1892. However, others claimed that the ghost continued to haunt the house well into the 20th century.

The SPR found no evidence of trickery, and the recurring, intelligent behaviour of the figure suggested an enduring identity—likely a ghost in the traditional sense.

What distinguished this case was the consistency of the apparition, the emotional tone it evoked, and the fact that it never interacted with the physical environment in any violent or unpredictable way. The Cheltenham haunting remains one of the most detailed and extensively witnessed ghost cases in British paranormal history.

Poltergeist or Ghost? The Crown Hotel Case (1966)

Type: Poltergeist activity combined with aspects of a traditional haunting, including the appearance of apparitions.

In the 1960s, the Crown Hotel in Poole, Dorset, began experiencing paranormal activity after the decision was made to convert an upper floor of a stable block into a 'beat' club. In 1966, two men who had been working in the club were talking to some customers in the courtyard when they all heard a piano—stored in an old first-floor room—being played. It sounded as if someone were striking the keys at random. One of the group joked that it could be a ghost. They decided to investigate and made their way upstairs to look inside the room. The room was empty, yet the disjointed notes could still be heard.

Suddenly, the workmen's tools—resting on top of the piano—shot into the air and clattered to the floor. Shocked, the group retreated to the courtyard, where they all saw a glowing ball of mist, about the size of a child's head, drift from the doorway of the piano room. It floated past them and glided through an archway leading to Market Street, where it vanished.

The sounds of something heavy being dragged across one of the upper floors were also heard in the hotel itself.

The old hayloft also appeared to be haunted. A secured door was seen opening on its own. A guest at the hotel who had heard of this dismissed it as nonsense and decided to paint five crosses on the door before bolting it. He was stunned to see the door slowly open before his eyes.

The hotel continued to be haunted. In 1974, the milkman refused to leave bottles in the courtyard, claiming he kept hearing the sounds of children running and screaming in the old stable block—a building he knew to be locked and empty. It later emerged that the hotel's owner had also once heard children's voices in the stable block. A search revealed no one present.

The ghost of a sad-looking young girl in a white nightdress was also seen leaning on a banister inside the hotel.

One guest reported seeing a blue light float from his bedroom, glide down the corridor, and vanish through a wall. Another guest once claimed to have been chatting with a man in the toilet when the man suddenly vanished. The guest was so shocked he had to be calmed down with a brandy.

No one is certain what lies behind the activity at the Crown Hotel, but a local legend states that in the 17th century, two disabled children were murdered by a former landlord in the stable block and buried under the floor of the larder. Until they receive a proper burial, their restless ghosts will haunt the building.

The strange events at the Crown Hotel blur the line between a traditional haunting and classic poltergeist activity. On one hand, there are unsettling reports of apparitions, eerie voices, and ghostly figures—hallmarks of a residual or intelligent haunting. On the other, the physical disturbances—objects flying, doors opening and a piano playing on its own—fit easily within the realm of poltergeist behaviour.

Categories help clarify our thinking—ghosts as personalities, poltergeists as chaotic energy—but many cases refuse to stay in their boxes. Some may begin as one type and gradually morph into another.

Chapter Fifteen
Interpreting the Unseen: Evidence and Argument in the Age of Spirits

As the 19th century dawned, society stood at a crossroads between tradition and modernity. Science was beginning to demystify the natural world, yet interest in the supernatural surged to unprecedented levels. It was during this era—marked by industrialisation, scientific discovery, and sweeping social change—that the poltergeist phenomenon evolved once again.

No longer confined to folklore or isolated rural households, reports of haunted parlours and intelligent spirits began to circulate in urban centres and middle-class drawing rooms. This transformation coincided with the rise of Spiritualism, a movement that claimed the dead could—and did—communicate with the living, often through mediums, séances, and automatic writing. Poltergeists, once feared as malicious entities, now became part of a broader conversation about the afterlife, consciousness, and the limits of human understanding.

However, some Victorian researchers and writers firmly rejected the idea that poltergeists were spirits and preferred alternative explanations. For instance, Catherine Crowe, author of *The Night Side of Nature*, suggested that poltergeists might be electrical in origin. She cited several cases in which mediums were said to give people electrical shocks even without touching them. Crowe also wrote of individuals under hypnosis who were able to produce an electrical shock through a simple act of will. If this were possible, she argued, then perhaps poltergeist phenomena could be caused by electrical energy. For example, was this how William Drury was able, as he claimed, to plague the Mompesson household in Tedworth? Yet such an ability still fails to account for all the phenomena associated with poltergeist hauntings.

Consider the case of the poltergeist that haunted the Reverend Phelps' home in Stratford, Connecticut. In March 1850, a visitor from New York suggested holding a séance, as the Phelps family had expressed interest in the subject. The attempt was unsuccessful, with only a few raps heard. A few days later, the family returned home to find the front door open and the house in disarray. It was assumed they had been burgled, but nothing appeared to have been taken.

That afternoon, the family went to church, while Reverend Phelps stayed behind to keep watch. He must have fallen asleep, because when the children returned, the house looked as though it had been ransacked—furniture was scattered, and in other rooms, clothes had been arranged to resemble people "in attitudes of extreme devotion," some with their foreheads nearly touching the floor. Open Bibles were spread out before them. Whatever was responsible appeared to be mocking the family's Christian devotions.

The following day, objects such as spoons, keys, bits of tin, and a bucket were seen flying through the air. A candlestick leapt from the mantelpiece and struck the floor repeatedly until it broke into pieces. There were also screams and a noise like someone attempting to destroy the house with an axe.

Two of the children, Harry (aged twelve) and Anna (aged sixteen), appeared to be the focus of the activity. Harry was once thrown into a cistern, and another time had his trousers torn from the bottom to above the knee. On one occasion, he was lifted into the air until his head nearly touched the ceiling.

The violence escalated, with the poltergeist smashing glass—including seventy-one windowpanes. It also appeared to attempt communication. Reverend Phelps would turn his back on his writing table, only to hear the sound of his pen scratching. When he examined his papers, he would find messages left for him. One such message read, "Very nice paper and ink for the devil."

Phelps attempted to communicate with the spirit through raps and believed there was more than one entity present. One claimed to be a French clerk who had once handled a settlement for Phelps and had since died. The spirit said he was now in hell for having cheated Phelps out of money. Upon investigation, the man's widow confirmed that her husband had indeed committed a minor fraud. On another occasion, the raps instructed Phelps to place his hand under the table. He complied—and was shocked to feel it grabbed by another hand, warm and seemingly human.

A psychic named Andrew Jackson Davis visited the Phelps home and proposed that the phenomena were caused by magnetism and electricity. He believed the magnetism was attracting objects to Harry and Anna, while the electricity caused items to fly away from them. Nevertheless, he also claimed to have seen five spirits present in the house.

The violence continued. Pieces of paper burst into flames, and various objects were smashed. Anna claimed to have been pinched while sitting with her mother and a reporter. When they rolled up her sleeve, they found a fresh pinch mark on her arm. On another occasion, a loud smacking sound was heard, and a red mark suddenly appeared on her cheek.

In October 1851, more than a year after the first outbreak, Mrs. Phelps and the four children moved to Pennsylvania for the winter. The poltergeist did not follow them, and after their return in spring, the house remained quiet.

Had Reverend Phelps unwittingly invited a spirit into his home by holding a séance—a popular Victorian method of communicating with the dead? And had the spirit discovered that it could manifest using the combined psychic energies of Anna and her brother Harry?

The Victorian fascination with spiritualism began in 1848, when the Fox family of Hydesville, New York, began experiencing strange phenomena in their home. At the time, the family consisted of John Fox, his wife Margaret, 10-year-old Kate, and 14-year-old Maggie. An older sister, Leah, and a brother, David, lived elsewhere. The first strange occurrence came in March 1848, when rapping sounds were heard in the house. The two sisters believed a ghost was responsible and nicknamed it "Mr. Splitfoot." They noticed that the raps mimicked the sound of them clapping their hands.

Mrs. Fox soon became involved. She asked the spirit to tap out the ages of her children, which it did—then added three extra raps. She was shaken, as she had once given birth to a child who had died at the age of three. The family devised a code: one rap for "yes," two for "no." Eventually, they developed an alphabetical code to determine the spirit's identity.

It claimed to be a peddler named Charles B. Rosna who had been murdered in the house five years earlier, his body buried in the cellar. When Mrs. Fox asked around, a maid who had worked there said that the former owner, John Bell, had once brought a man home who vanished the next day. She had assumed the man had left early.

John Bell, upon hearing these claims, was furious and accused the Foxes of lying. The police investigated but found no records of a missing peddler. However, in 1904, a wall in the cellar collapsed, revealing several bones—though some claimed they were animal remains. A tin box, allegedly belonging to the murdered peddler, was also discovered.

Other phenomena followed. The family heard gurgling noises and the sound of dragging across the floor. Even when separated, the rapping sounds followed the sisters. Pins were jabbed into praying family members, and Mrs. Fox once had a comb pulled from her hair. The raps became thunderous, like cannon fire.

Eventually, a spirit delivered a message: "Dear friends, you must proclaim this truth to the world. This is the dawning of a new era." With this proclamation, spiritualism was born.

All three Fox sisters became mediums. During séances, participants would sit around a table while the sisters summoned spirits who communicated through raps, vibrations, or table movements. Soon, the sisters were touring American theatres, with large crowds eager to witness their communications with the dead. Within months, spiritualism spread across America and then to Europe.

In 1888, the Fox sisters shocked the spiritualist community by admitting they had faked the phenomena. A newspaper had offered $1,500 for a confession, and Maggie took the offer. Kate, however, remained silent.

By this time, their careers had declined. Kate was struggling with alcoholism, and Maggie had undergone a crisis of faith, converting to Catholicism. Kate later denounced Maggie's confession, while Maggie herself eventually retracted it, claiming the original manifestations had been genuine. The later fakery, she said, was orchestrated by Leah, who wanted to maintain the family's income after the genuine phenomena had ceased. Maggie also defended other mediums, asserting that their work was valid and sincere.

The Fox Sisters.

Despite the controversy, spiritualism continued to flourish. By the early 20th century, it had attracted millions of followers worldwide.

Whether it's a sceptic who sees only deception or a believer who sees spirits at work, the lens through which we view the poltergeist is often shaped by our personal experiences, beliefs, and biases. Poltergeist phenomena do not adhere to simple patterns, and attempts to categorise them too narrowly risk missing the complexity of these cases.

In the next chapter, we will show how personal bias—whether scientific, or emotional—can also profoundly influence the way poltergeist cases are understood.

Chapter Sixteen

Theories, Myths, and Misconceptions

The Society for Psychical Research (SPR) was formed in 1882 to investigate and understand paranormal activity. The founders of the SPR hoped that the debate over the paranormal—including the existence of ghosts—would eventually reach a definitive conclusion. However, this was not to be the case. As the modern investigator knows, studying the subject is not as straightforward as our Victorian forebears believed. Ghosts and poltergeists do not appear on demand and show no inclination to cooperate with human beings. To frustrate the investigator, they often refuse to appear at all—or, worse, cause chaos and confusion when they do.

One of the biggest mistakes in poltergeist research is that we often impose our own biases onto the phenomenon's cause. In the past, we blamed demons, fairies, witches, or ghosts. Today, we blame telekinesis or fraud. Indeed, for many scientists, trickery and fraud are the only acceptable explanations. Hans J. Eysenck and Carl Sargent provide an example of this rigid mindset in their book *Explaining the Unexplained*. After one lecture at the Royal Institution on PK metal bending, a physicist, his face purple with rage, jumped up and shouted, "It's all nonsense. Nonsense. Heard it all before. It's nonsense." On another occasion, a colleague of Sargent's, after hearing a presentation on ESP, was overheard saying, "The results you presented would convince me of anything else but this. I just cannot believe it, and I don't know why."

Derren Brown, a well-known sceptic who can replicate many paranormal effects on stage, also comes to mind. However, the fact that such phenomena can be reproduced by illusion does not mean all paranormal events are mere trickery. One wonders what Brown would make of the 19th-century medium Daniel Douglas Home, who was repeatedly witnessed levitating tables and even floating up to the ceiling. Standing against a wall, his legs and waist restrained, Home could increase his height by eight inches. He reportedly removed red-hot coals from a fireplace and handed them to others, who found them merely warm. He even placed his head in open flames without injury.

Daniel Douglas Home.

W. Stainton Moses, an Anglican priest and spiritualist, witnessed this:

"[Mr. Home] then went to the fireplace, removed the guard, and sat down on the hearthrug. There, he seemed to hold a conversation by signs with a spirit. He repeatedly bowed and finally set to work to mesmerise his head again. He ruffled his bushy hair until it stood out like a mop, and then deliberately lay down and put his head in the bright wood fire. The hair was in the blaze, and must, under ordinary circumstances, have been singed off. His head was in the grate, and his neck on a level with the top bar. This was repeated several times. He also put his hand into the fire, smoothed away the wood and coal, and picked up a live coal, which he held in his hand for a few seconds, but replaced soon, saying the power was not sufficient."

Home was also said to levitate at will. James Lindsay, later Earl of Crawford and Balcarres, described one such event in 1868:

"Mr. Home went into a trance, and in that state was carried out of a window in the room next to where we were and was brought in at our window. The distance between the windows was about 7 ft 6 in, and there was not the slightest foothold between them, nor more than a 12-inch projection to each window, which served as a ledge to put flowers on. We heard the window in the next room lifted up, and almost immediately after, we saw Home floating in the air outside our window. The moon was shining full into the room; my back was to the light, and I saw the shadow on the wall of the window sill, and Home's feet about six feet above it. He remained in this position a few seconds, then raised the window and glided into the room, feet foremost, and sat down. Lord Adare then went into the next room to look at the window from which he had been carried, it was raised about 18 inches, and he expressed his wonder how Mr. Home had been taken through so narrow an aperture. Home said (still in trance). 'I will show you; and then, with his back to the window, he leaned back, and was shot out of the aperture head first with the body rigid, and then returned quite quietly. The window is about 70 feet from the ground. I very much doubt whether any skilful tight-rope dancer would like to attempt a feat of this description, where the only means of crossing would be by a perilous leap or being borne across in such a manner as I have described."

Harry Houdini, known for debunking spiritualists and séances, called Home a fraud and claimed he could duplicate his feats—but never demonstrated that he had done so. Remarkably, Home was never exposed in any of his 1,500 séances as committing fraud.

Today, despite the many theories surrounding poltergeists, one fact remains clear: the "focus person" in a poltergeist case is not always a troubled female adolescent. Men can also be the epicentre.

In 1965, actor Brian Cox was 19 and appearing in a play at The Royal Lyceum in Edinburgh. While renting a room on Comely Bank Road, he heard tapping sounds and saw a chair shaking. The chair began to move across the floor toward him. Terrified, he hid under the bedcovers until morning. When he emerged, he found the chair beside his bed, with scratch marks on the floor showing its path.

Dr. William Roll, Director of Research at the Psychical Research Foundation in North Carolina, found that of all poltergeist cases reported before 1900, about 80% involved a female focus. But by the 20th century, this gender gap had narrowed, suggesting that the theory linking poltergeists to repressed female sexuality was overly simplistic. Roll also noted that a disproportionate number of individuals involved in poltergeist activity exhibited symptoms similar to those of epilepsy. During an epileptic seizure, powerful electrical discharges occur in the brain. Could this energy, as Roll proposed, manifest externally—causing objects to move, fires to ignite, and raps to echo through walls?

Roll further observed that the average age of the focus person initially hovered around 16 but later shifted to 20. Other studies have shown that the focus can be a middle-aged man or woman, or even someone in their 70s.

It is now widely accepted that more than one person can act as an energy source in a poltergeist event. In some cases, as we have previously shown, the individual thought to be at the centre of the disturbance is removed from the location, yet the activity continues. As authors John and Anne Spencer observed: "Just because it is clear one individual is the focus of the poltergeist, it does not necessarily mean that only one individual is responsible."

However, it remains evident that many poltergeist cases are linked to emotionally unstable households. Often, at least one family member suffers from anxiety, depression, frustration, sexual tension, or even mental illness. Roll noted: "The red thread running through most of the cases I have investigated or am familiar with is tension in family situations or extensions of them."

This tension often originates from deprivation, neglect, or a deep-seated desire for attention. Roll discovered that in 62% of the cases he studied, the focus person was away from home when the outbreak began. Among the rest, 17% lived in single-parent households.

Chapter Seventeen
Pete the Poltergeist

One of the most intriguing poltergeist hauntings on record took place at a small premises named Mower Services in Cardiff. Established in the late 1970s by John and Pat Matthews, along with Pat's brother Fred Cook, the business—selling and repairing lawnmowers—consisted of a workshop and a small yard set back from Crwys Road. For hundreds of years, the beginning of Crwys Road, marking the boundary between Cardiff and Roath, was used for executions. Even today, the road junction is known as "Death Junction."

Mower Services had originally formed part of a row of terraced houses built in the early 1880s. By the 20th century, the area had become a busy residential and commercial district to the north of the city centre, with numerous shops, a bank, a school, and a Baptist church.

The haunting started with stones being thrown onto the metal roof of the building. It was assumed that local children were responsible, but John, despite running outside, was unable to find them. The problem began to worsen, with the stones now hitting the windows, and the Matthews decided to inform the police, who failed to catch the culprits.

The situation worsened further, with the workshop also becoming affected. The staff saw stones, bolts, and ball bearings flying across the room and hitting the walls. The objects even targeted members of the staff, but fortunately, no one suffered any injuries. As the phenomenon intensified, the Matthews quickly discarded their initial assumption that someone in the building was playing a practical joke.

A paint scraper vanished, only to reappear so hot to the touch that a blowlamp could have heated it. A terrible burning smell would follow the sudden icy coldness in one corner of the workshop. A lawn mower suddenly started up on its own, smashed dishes miraculously repaired themselves, and dust was dropped down the backs of workmen's shirts. A diary once vanished from a drawer, only to reappear on the roof of an adjacent building. One day, a set of keys vanished, and as everyone searched for them, they unexpectedly materialised and shot across the floor.

The Matthews were also plagued by phone calls to their home, sometimes every few minutes, but there was never anyone at the other end of the line. The couple called out telephone engineers, but they were unable to locate any fault with the system.

The Matthews decided to lock up the building and have the staff stand around a bench. They then instructed each of them to hold out their hands to prevent any potential deceit. John asked for a stone to be thrown. A stone suddenly fell on the table. One of the others suggested writing down what had happened. In response, a pen fell to the floor, followed by a sheet of headed notepaper from the office on the first floor. Someone requested a spark plug, which promptly fell onto the table.

Fred Cook then asked for a gold sovereign. A coin from Queen Elizabeth II's Silver Jubilee suddenly appeared. John recognised the coin—he usually kept it in a drawer at his home. In all, the session in the workshop lasted for two hours.

Following this display, the staff decided to nickname the poltergeist "Pete." The Matthews now decided to call in David Fontana, a professor of psychology at Cardiff University and a member of the Society for Psychical Research. He later became its president from 1995 to 1998. Fontana's investigation of the case would last from June 1989 to early 1992.

The professor's first visit proved to be an eventful one.

As the investigator entered the workshop, a stone was suddenly thrown across the room and bounced off a piece of machinery. John, who was sitting nearby talking to one of the sales representatives, made it clear that neither he nor the representative was involved in the incident. John looked up at the investigator and said, "There—see what I mean? He's greeting you." Professor Fontana felt a sense of satisfaction, as such occurrences were rare for investigators to witness firsthand. This experience led him to take the situation much more seriously than he might have otherwise.

Typically, in poltergeist cases, one hears objects hit the wall and clatter to the ground, but rarely does one see the object mid-air. In this case, the stone was found on the floor after the noise, but its flight had not been observed. This, the investigator thought, only reinforced the idea that no one was playing tricks—if they were, the stone would have been seen in flight.

Professor Fontana was impressed by the incident and made several return visits, usually unannounced. The poltergeist appeared to delight in throwing things at Fontana, such as a stone and a ball bearing. He also observed the disappearance and reappearance of a coin, and the sudden appearance of a pen when Pete was requested to bring one. Fontana also observed "active corners" in the building, where the poltergeist would return objects thrown to him.

The professor witnessed an incident that had the potential to cause a serious injury. Pat Matthews had entered the workshop from the adjoining retail shop.

As she was closing the door behind her, a large strimming wheel smashed against it. As Fontana noted, "Had the object arrived a split second sooner, it would in all probability have struck her a serious blow on the back of the head."

A brass shell case weighing 25 pounds flew across the workshop several times, and John decided to remove it to the yard. Later, while working at his bench, the case fell beside him. When the poltergeist was ordered to "fire the shell," blue flames were seen to emerge from it.

The case quickly garnered media attention and was covered in several newspapers, including *Wales on Sunday*, which featured the story with the headline, *Haunted and Taunted by Pete the Poltergeist*. Speaking about the poltergeist, John said, "It seems to stem from one corner. One day I was moving things about in that particular corner, and because I was disturbing him, he threw two big marbles which just missed me."

One man worked just two doors from Mower Services. He had heard about the poltergeist and was not convinced it was a genuine haunting. One day, walking past the premises, he decided to throw a stone into the yard. He was shocked when the stone was thrown back and landed at his feet. Interestingly, the stone had failed to hit the metal door, which had been its intended target.

Pat and John were worried that the poltergeist would frighten away customers, but their fears were unfounded, as customers were keen to witness the poltergeist for themselves. One, Joyce Glenn, observed nuts and bolts flying around and dropping on the floor out of nowhere. Another was showered with manure, prompting him to flee the building without waiting for his change!

The phenomenon continued. A table in the kitchen at the back of the premises was often found crudely laid out with cutlery and cups. Once, John joked to Pat, "We've had everything except wood." He had barely finished his sentence when he saw a plank of wood flying into the shop. It travelled with such force that it took a piece out of an adjoining door.

Once, thieves forced open the front door of the building and stole £1,200 worth of stock. The insurance company sent Gareth Lucas to assess the claim. While visiting the shop, he heard stones being thrown at the back of the building. Curious, he asked the staff about it and was casually told, "Oh, that's Pete the Poltergeist." At first, he didn't believe them—but when he opened the door and looked through, he saw a stone spinning on the floor. There was no one else there.

One of his colleagues, Reg Jenkin, was sceptical, but he decided to visit the premises using the excuse that he wished to conduct a fire risk survey. He also witnessed stones being thrown about.

Pete the Poltergeist could also prove generous. Upon opening the building, staff would find a £5 or £10 note stuck to the ceiling tiles. Fred Cook even found one note pasted to the wet windscreen of his car. In all, they found £70. Coins, including old pennies, would also appear, dropping at the feet of the person who had requested them. One coin was found to date from 1912.

Pete would also visit the home of Fred, where he would throw £1 coins at the front door as Fred crossed the hallway. Carburettor floats, which control the petrol flow in lawnmower engines, were found lodged in ceilings. Once, Fred, his wife, and her sister were relaxing in the garden when the needle end of a carburettor float was pushed through the top of their parasol.

John Matthews once challenged the poltergeist to move a carburettor float left on a flat surface in the workshop. As he was locking up for the evening, he felt something in his hand. Opening it, he saw the needle end of the float resting in his palm.

The poltergeist was even active in a nearby charity shop. Christine Windels was shocked to see a piece of string coming through the ceiling. It came through, curled back on itself, and then dropped to the floor. She looked up at the ceiling, but there were no holes to explain its sudden appearance.

The Baptist church, next door to the lawnmower business, also experienced some poltergeist activity. One evening, the Reverend Mike Fuller was working in his office when stones started hitting the window. He went outside but could see no one. Interestingly, the stone-throwing stopped after Mike and members of his congregation walked around the boundary of the church and prayed.

In 1991, Fred Cook saw an apparition. Upon opening the door to the workshop, he saw a small boy sitting on a shelf near the ceiling. He appeared to be dressed in clothing typical of the 1940s. He wore what looked like a cub cap on his head. The outlines of his hands and face were visible, and yet no clear facial features could be made out. It was as if his entire form was grey—there was a face, but at the same time, there wasn't. He was sitting on a sort of fixture used to store spare parts for lawnmowers. What stood out was how out of proportion he seemed. His body didn't match his scale—his head should have reached the ceiling. The overall impression was of something physically distorted, something not quite right.

Fred called out, "Hello! What are you doing here?" The apparition did not speak and threw a carburettor at him. The figure then vanished.

Pete would appear again. On its second appearance, John and Fred were working on a mower in the workshop. Fred saw the boy sitting on the shelf. He told John to turn around slowly and look, but as he did so, a house brick was thrown at the mower.

So who was Pete? It was suggested that the apparition was a seven-year-old boy who had died in a car accident near the workshop. Afterwards, a woman came forward who said that her brother was the boy involved in the fatal accident. However, Fred Cook wondered if the poltergeist was connected to his deceased father, as some of the coins that appeared bore the year of his father's birth. Whatever the explanation, John Matthews believed the poltergeist was childish in its behaviour and just wanted to play.

Fred once spotted the apparition of the boy sitting on the counter next to the till. He was swinging his legs. As Fred walked towards him, the boy faded away. Later, as Fred was locking up, the apparition appeared again. It stood before him, illuminated by the light from an open washroom door, and seemed to be waving goodbye.

He wore boots up to his ankles, a short coat, and a small cub cap perched on his head. His appearance was entirely grey, as though drained of all colour. He had no discernible face—yet somehow, a face seemed to be there. It was difficult to explain. The only clear movement was his hand, slowly waving.

In 1993, Mower Services moved to a new industrial estate in Cardiff. The old workshop was later demolished. The retail section of the premises became a restaurant. There have never been any reports of paranormal activity there.

The poltergeist moved to Fred Cook's home. It would turn small pictures in their frames and toss spoons upstairs. Once, a small blue jug vanished and then reappeared four days later. The Cooks finally decided to move. The couple smashed the jug, as they did not want the poltergeist to follow them to their new home. The destruction of the jug had the desired effect, as Pete the Poltergeist never reappeared.

Sceptics of the case are quick to blame the haunting on the alleged gullibility of witnesses, who, for instance, mistook the vibrations of traffic, the activity of rodents, or children throwing stones as paranormal activity. Others believe that a staff member faked the poltergeist to scare their co-workers. However, Professor Fontana rejected such explanations in his report to the Society for Psychical Research, entitled *A Responsive Poltergeist: A Case from South Wales*. He had, after all, witnessed some of the phenomena himself. He also conducted experiments at the workshop, throwing a stone into a corner; the poltergeist would then throw it back to him. He noted that although he witnessed objects being thrown, he never saw their flight through the air—only the moment they landed. As we have previously noted, the failure of witnesses to see objects in flight has frequently been reported in poltergeist cases. This, for Fontana, reinforced the legitimacy of the case. He was also impressed with the integrity of the witnesses, whom he regarded as reliable and sincere. The activity witnessed in nearby properties was also compelling. Fontana believed that the poltergeist possessed intent and rudimentary intelligence. He did not believe it was a hoax.

Professor David Fontana died in 2010 after a long and distinguished career as a psychologist, parapsychologist, and author. He never wavered from the conviction that the Cardiff haunting was an authentic manifestation of the poltergeist phenomenon. The Matthews and Fred Cook also remained convinced that they had witnessed genuine poltergeist activity, dismissing any notions that they had been victims of a hoax perpetrated by someone working in the workshop.

The Mower Services case stands as one of the most compelling and multifaceted poltergeist hauntings ever recorded in Britain. What makes it so striking isn't just the sheer volume of bizarre events—from flying tools to a seemingly sentient presence—but the presence of credible witnesses and a seasoned investigator who was able to observe the phenomenon firsthand.

Professor Fontana's long-term involvement provided a rare level of scientific scrutiny to what is often a fleeting and elusive phenomenon. His reports not only documented the chaotic occurrences but also highlighted the consistency and intelligence behind the activity. This wasn't just a random barrage of events. Pete, as the poltergeist came to be affectionately known, responded to requests, and occasionally exhibited humour and generosity.

This case again blurs the lines between traditional hauntings and poltergeist phenomena. Traditionally, hauntings involve residual energy or sentient spirits linked to a particular place, often repeating past events or appearing as apparitions. Poltergeist activity, on the other hand, is typically associated with disruptive energy— usually chaotic and short-lived.

Yet here we see elements of both: a ghostly, child-like figure with a clear physical form; items that vanish and reappear with intent; and a presence that follows people from one location to another. Pete wasn't confined to the workshop—he followed Fred Cook home and even interacted with his family, displaying behaviour that was often playful but occasionally unsettling.

In many ways, the Mower Services case challenges the neat categories often used in paranormal research. It suggests that what we call "poltergeists" might not always be a single phenomenon. Some may be residual psychic energy, others mischievous spirits, and still others something else entirely—intelligent, interactive, and capable of forming attachments to people and places.

Whether Pete was the spirit of a lost child, a psychic imprint, or an elemental force of mischief, his legacy remains one of the most puzzling and enduring in the annals of British paranormal history.

Chapter Eighteen
The Enfield Case

While the events at Mower Services in Cardiff were remarkable for their intensity and duration, they were also notable for occurring in a commercial setting—far from the domestic environments typically associated with poltergeist disturbances. Yet despite the unusual location, many of the features were strikingly familiar: objects thrown without visible cause, strange noises, electrical disturbances, and a sense of intelligence behind the activity.

These recurring elements appear again and again in poltergeist cases across decades and continents, suggesting a shared pattern that transcends individual circumstance. One of the most famous—and most fiercely debated—of these cases is the Enfield Poltergeist. Occurring before "Pete" made himself known in Cardiff, the Enfield case brought poltergeist activity into the public spotlight like never before. But unlike the business-like setting of Mower Services, this haunting unfolded in a modest council house and focused on a family already under considerable strain.

What follows is a closer look at the Enfield case: a haunting that captured headlines, divided experts, and remains one of the most controversial episodes in the history of psychical research.

In the 1970s, the town of Enfield in North London garnered international attention due to the apparent activity of a poltergeist at a property located at 284 Green Street. The family living in the 1920s semi-detached council house consisted of Mrs. Peggy Hodgson and her four children: Margaret, thirteen; Janet, eleven; Johnny, ten; and Billy, seven.

The haunting began on the evening of August 30, 1977. Johnny and Janet shared a bedroom, and just after they had gone to bed, their beds started to shake violently. Calling out to their mother, the shaking abruptly stopped. Mrs. Hodgson, assuming they were playing games, told them firmly to get some sleep. The following evening, the children heard a shuffling sound in their room. When Mrs. Hodgson entered and told them to be quiet, she also heard the shuffling. Then, four loud knocks followed. Turning on the light, she was startled to see a heavy chest of drawers sliding across the floor toward the door. Mrs. Hodgson pushed it back to its normal position, but the furniture moved again toward the doorway. This time, despite her efforts, she was unable to push it back. Scared, she quickly took the children downstairs.

Seeking help, Mrs. Hodgson went next door to ask her neighbours. Vic Nottingham and his son accompanied her to search the house but found nothing unusual. When they heard a knocking sound, Vic rushed outside to see if someone was banging on the wall. However, there was no one to be found.

On Thursday, September 1, Mrs. Hodgson decided to call the police. Local officers, WPC Heeps and PC Hyams arrived at approximately 1:00 a.m. Upon arrival, they found several individuals gathered in the living room of the house. Mrs Hodgson explained that strange occurrences had been taking place over the previous nights and that they suspected the house might be haunted.

Accompanied by Hyams, Heeps entered the living room. The lights were turned off, and almost immediately, they heard a series of four distinct knocks coming from the wall that adjoined the neighbouring property. After a brief silence, another set of four taps was heard—this time from a different wall. PC Hyams and neighbours conducted a thorough check of the walls, attic, and plumbing, but found nothing that could account for the sounds.

Later, Hyams and the neighbours moved into the kitchen to inspect the refrigerator and pipework, leaving the policewoman alone in the living room with the family. The lights were once again switched off, leaving the room illuminated only by the streetlights outside. Within minutes, the family's eldest son pointed toward a chair situated near the sofa. Heeps observed the chair wobbling slightly from side to side before it began to slide across the floor, moving three to four feet towards the kitchen wall before coming to a stop. At no point did the chair appear to lift off the ground.

Heeps examined the chair but found no explanation for how it had moved. The lights were turned back on, and no further incidents occurred during the remainder of the visit.

After the police left, the family decided to stay in the living room. They enjoyed a quiet day until the evening, when they witnessed Lego bricks and marbles flying around the room. They found the marbles to be hot when they picked them up.

Mrs. Hodgson agreed to have her neighbour call the *Daily Mirror*, which sent over a reporter and a photographer. Nothing happened initially, and the pair decided to leave. However, as they were leaving, Lego bricks and marbles began flying about the room again. Mrs. Hodgson called them back, and as they returned, a Lego brick struck the photographer above his right eye. The newspaper then decided to approach the Society for Psychical Research (SPR). They contacted Maurice Grosse, who had recently joined the SPR and was keen to investigate a case. Then, Guy Lyon Playfair, another SPR member, also became involved in the investigation.

At first, Playfair suspected Janet of being responsible, as she appeared quite lively. He instructed Mrs. Hodgson to monitor Janet closely and informed her, "Even if Janet is deceiving, it might not be her fault." Playfair had found that often the 'focus' in a poltergeist case would throw things without being aware of it. In one case, for instance, a person was caught throwing objects, but a lie detector test indicated the individual believed they were telling the truth when they denied it.

Margaret Hodgson.
Photo: Guy Lyon Playfair Estate.

Playfair and the *Mirror* photographer were waiting in Janet's bedroom when a marble landed on the floor. Playfair observed that the marble did not roll upon landing but remained stationary. He tried to replicate this but was unable to do so. The photographer attempted to take a picture, but all the flash guns on his cameras failed.

Upon checking them, he discovered they had inexplicably run out of power.

Playfair decided to tie the leg of Janet's chair to her bed using wire. Despite this, the chair fell over, and the wire snapped. He watched as an armchair also toppled over and the bed slid across the floor. A book titled *Fun and Games for Children* flew off a shelf and landed upright on the floor. A small head-like indentation appeared on a pillow. Mrs. Hodgson suggested to Playfair that this was caused by the ghost of a four-year-old girl, smothered by her father in a nearby house. Some furniture from that house had ended up in the Hodgsons' home, but Mrs. Hodgson had since discarded it.

Knocks were heard, and Playfair thought the poltergeist was attempting to communicate. A medium, Annie Shaw, visited the house with her husband, George. She entered a trance and became upset, screaming, "Go away!" and spitting at her husband. She moaned, "Gozer, Gozer, help me. Elvie, come here." George asked the entity to leave the Hodgson family alone.

Annie came out of the trance and claimed Janet was the centre of the haunting, asserting that more than one entity was involved. She said that both Janet's and her mother's auric fields were leaking and that the entities were using this energy to manifest. She also sensed a negative atmosphere in the house. Mrs. Hodgson admitted she still felt bitter towards her ex-husband.

George added that 'Gozer' was a practitioner of black magic and 'Elvie' was an elemental. The Shaws then 'cleaned' Janet's and her mother's auras by moving their hands over their bodies.

For a few weeks, the activity almost ceased. However, in October, the poltergeist returned. Beds shook, furniture moved, and blankets flew off beds. Pools of water appeared on the kitchen floor—one even resembled a human figure. The poltergeist grew more violent. On one occasion, an iron grille from a fireplace flew across the room and hit Billy's pillow. Had it struck him, it could have killed him. The following evening, a gas fire was torn out of the wall.

On the advice of fellow researcher E.J. Dingwall, Playfair attempted to communicate with the poltergeist. Using raps, it rapped back. He asked it to rap once for yes and twice for no. When he asked if the entity realised it was dead, loud crashes echoed from an upstairs bedroom. Rushing upstairs, he found objects scattered across the floor.

Maurice Grosse also attempted communication. He asked if it had died in the house, and it rapped 'Yes.' He then asked if it would go away, to which a loud thud replied 'No.' The poltergeist claimed to have lived in the house for over thirty years. When the raps became nonsensical, Grosse asked if it was playing a game with him. In response, a cardboard box containing cushions flew across the room and hit him on the forehead. Playfair, standing outside the door, recorded the incident on tape. Strangely, no one had seen the box flying—it was as if it had dematerialised and then rematerialised upon impact.

The children then began to see apparitions. Billy claimed to have seen a disembodied face staring at him—an old man with large, white teeth.

As time went on, the poltergeist grew increasingly violent. It flung Janet eight feet across the room and grabbed Margaret. The investigators later found her upstairs, standing on one leg with the other stretched behind her, unable to move. She could only walk again when Grosse twisted her sideways.

They asked the poltergeist to write a message using pen and paper. A few minutes later, they found: "I will stay in the house. Do not show this to anyone, or I will retaliate." Another message was more mundane: "Can I have a tea bag?" Mrs. Hodgson placed a tea bag on the table, and moments later, a second one appeared beside it. When her ex-husband visited and she showed him the message, she remembered the warning. She apologised aloud. A new message appeared: "A misunderstanding. Don't do it again."

The SPR sent a team of investigators who appeared inclined to dismiss the case as a hoax. Playfair and Grosse were unimpressed with their apparent lack of impartiality.

Janet remained the focal point. She was thrown out of bed and once found asleep on top of a radio set. She went into convulsions, screamed hysterically, and wandered around saying, "Where's Gober? He'll kill you."

Playfair invited two Brazilian mediums, Luiz Gasparetto and Elsie Dubugras, who believed Janet was a powerful medium. One of them wrote: "I see this child, Janet, in the Middle Ages—a cruel and wanton woman who caused suffering to families of yeomen. Some of these want to get even with the family."

In December 1977, the poltergeist began speaking through Janet. It started by whistling and barking but eventually formed words, calling out Maurice's name. It identified itself as Bill Wilkins. When asked if he knew he was dead, he told Playfair to "shut up." At first, he would not speak if investigators were present. The voice claimed it had a dog named "Gober the Ghost" and shook Janet's bed because it wanted her out. It used foul language and said it enjoyed annoying them. When asked where it came from, it replied, "I come from out the grave," and named a local cemetery—Durant's Park. Asked why it didn't go away, it said, "I'm not a heaven man. I come from Durant's Park. I am seventy-two years old. I came here to see my family, but they are not here now." Bill later claimed he had gone blind and died in a chair downstairs—information later confirmed through research. When Playfair asked why he wasn't visible, Bill said, "I'm invisible… because I'm a G.H.O.S.T."

To rule out fakery, Grosse taped Janet's mouth—but the voice continued. He had her hold water in her mouth—the voice continued to speak. He even placed a microphone on the back of her head to record it. A speech therapist concluded that the voice might originate from the false vocal cords, though prolonged use typically causes throat damage—none of which Janet showed, even after speaking for hours. Was she merely an amplifier?

"The tape recordings of this spirit," wrote Colin Wilson, "sound oddly hoarse and breathless, as if the voice is not being produced in the normal way by vocal cords and lungs." Accusations of ventriloquism prompted Grosse to offer a £1,000 reward to anyone who could replicate the voice under the same conditions. No one claimed the prize.

Another researcher, David Robertson, became involved. He asked the poltergeist to levitate Janet and draw a line around a ceiling light. He left the room and soon heard Janet bouncing on the bed. A gasp followed—then silence. The door was jammed shut. Upon opening it, Janet was on the bed. Looking up, Robertson saw a red line around the light. Janet claimed to have floated through the wall into the bedroom next door. When neighbour Peggy Nottingham asked her to do it again, Janet failed to appear, but a book—*Fun and Games for Children*—was found in the room. It had been in Janet's room minutes earlier.

Robertson gave Janet a red cushion and asked her to do something with it. The voice said, "All right, David, boy. I'll make it disappear." He stepped out of the room, but then heard Janet shout. When he came back, the cushion was gone. Not long before that, a neighbour walking by had seen a red cushion appear on the roof.

Playfair thought Janet might have had an out-of-body experience. He pointed out that she described Peggy's bedroom as "all white," which matched what others had said after similar experiences—they often noticed a lack of colour. Still, that doesn't explain how Janet's book ended up in Peggy's room.

Hazel Short, the local lollipop lady, once claimed to have dramatically witnessed Janet floating around her room. She said she had been standing outside, looking at the house, when suddenly a couple of books flew across the room and hit the window. It startled her, especially because it was so quiet at the time—there was no traffic, and the noise made her jump.

A short while later, Hazel said she saw Janet. She wasn't sure if there was a bed under the window, but Janet appeared to be rising and falling in the air, as if someone were tossing her up and down in a horizontal position—like someone had hold of her legs and back and was throwing her. Hazel said she clearly saw Janet reach the height of the window and noted that if Janet had been bouncing, it would have made more sense for her to push off her feet. She didn't believe Janet could have bounced that high off her back. Hazel also mentioned that a friend who was with her at the time saw the same thing.

The second witness was John Rainbow, a baker who was delivering bread to the school across the street at the time.

He said that before that day, he never believed any of the stories, even though he'd heard all the rumours about strange things happening in the house. But what he saw changed his mind. He described seeing the child floating around the room while the curtains blew inward, even though the windows were shut tight. He said she seemed to be spinning slowly in a clockwise direction.

At one point, her arm banged against the window twice, and he was genuinely scared. He thought she might crash through the glass and fall onto the road. "I was frightened," he said. "There's no doubt about it."

Playfair tried to replicate the levitation by bouncing on the bed horizontally but was unsuccessful.

Playfair and Grosse decided to hypnotise Janet. Dr. Ian Fletcher, a hypnotist and member of the Magic Circle, was called in:

Q: Do you know who is doing all this?

A: *Me and my sister.*

Q: Why do you think you are to blame?

A: *I don't know who is.*

Q: What does it feel like?

A: *Cold hands gripping me, gripping me around my body.*

Q: Who started the trouble?

A: *None of us.*

Q: What is the cause of the trouble?

A: *An increase in unhappiness.*

Fletcher was impressed. "This is not fraud. She and her sister are doing some of these things, maybe springing out of bed. Something is forcing them to do it against their will."

American paranormal investigators Ed and Lorraine Warren made an unannounced visit and became convinced the events were supernatural. Their brief visit inspired the film *The Conjuring 2*—a highly fictionalised account of the haunting.

Janet remained the 'focus' of the poltergeist. At one point, it attempted to strangle her with the curtains and made a knife float behind her. This time, the voice claimed another entity, named Tommy, was responsible. A biscuit appeared from nowhere and was shoved into Janet's mouth. Small fires began breaking out in closed drawers, and the house became filled with appalling smells—like rotten cabbage. Two pet goldfish were found dead, the poltergeist claiming to have electrocuted them by accident. The family's pet parakeet was also discovered dead in its cage. Obscene messages began appearing on the kitchen wall.

A visiting medium, Gerry Sherrick, told the family they had been together in past lives and that the girls had once practiced witchcraft. He also said an old woman was connected to the haunting—a woman who had lived near Spitalfields Market in London. He then asked if the family had experienced the smell of rotten vegetables. They confirmed this. Sherrick entered a trance, and an old woman's voice emerged: "I'm not bleeding dead, and I'm not going to go away." He offered the family psychic healing to seal the "leaks" that had caused the haunting.

Following his visit, the house remained quiet for several weeks. When the poltergeist activity resumed, it was far less intense. Mrs. Hodgson reported seeing a ghostly pair of legs in blue trousers ascending the stairs. She also saw the apparition of a child, and the children claimed to have seen the ghost of an old man. A neighbour who was watching the house during the Hodgsons' absence saw an apparition of a man in shirtsleeves sitting at a table. Another neighbour, knocking at the door, saw Maurice Grosse walking upstairs through the glass. When she entered the house, she found that Grosse had already been upstairs for half an hour. She had apparently seen his doppelgänger.

Midway through 1978, Janet was admitted to Maudsley Hospital for observation. During her absence, the activity continued, though at a much-reduced level. Janet claimed the poltergeist had caused disturbances in the hospital as well.

A visit by another medium, Dono Gmelig-Meyling, appeared to mark the end of the haunting. He told Playfair about his 'astral trip,' during which he encountered a 24-year-old girl connected to the case. He sensed a strong connection between Maurice Grosse and the haunting. Grosse revealed that his daughter, also named Janet, had died in a motorcycle accident two years earlier. She would have been 24 at the time. Dono responded, "Well, that's it. It's your daughter." However, he clarified that this didn't mean she was responsible for the haunting—only that she had helped draw Grosse into the case.

Grosse recalled several peculiar incidents surrounding his daughter's death. The day before her fatal accident, she had sent her brother a birthday card featuring a character with a head injury. She had jokingly written a message referencing it— she died from a head injury.

Grosse had wondered whether his daughter's spirit truly existed. He believed rain would be a sign, as there had been a prolonged drought. The next morning, he found the kitchen roof wet—right below her old bedroom window—while the rest of the area remained dry. It was Janet's death that had led Grosse to begin working in psychical research. His first case was the Enfield haunting.

Playfair concluded that tensions in the Hodgson home had triggered the phenomenon:

"When Mr. and Mrs. Hodgson were divorced, an atmosphere of tension built among the children and their mother, just at the time when the two girls were approaching physical maturity. They were a very energetic pair to start with, both of them school sports champions, but even they could not use up the tremendous energy they were generating. So a number of entities came in and helped themselves to it."

In 2003, Peggy Hodgson died at 284 Green Street. She was 73. "She didn't want to move," explained her daughter, Margaret. "She said, 'It ain't going to kill me, so I may as well stay here until I die.'" Margaret also claimed her mother continued to experience poltergeist activity: "Doors and drawers would open and close on their own. There were knocking sounds. She'd put a book down in one room, and it would appear in another."

After Peggy's death, the house was briefly occupied by Clare Bennett, who said: "I didn't see anything, but I felt uncomfortable. There was definitely some kind of presence in the house—I always felt like someone was looking at me." Her children would wake at night, claiming to hear people talking downstairs. Clare later discovered the house's history. "Suddenly, it all made sense," she said. They moved out after just two months.

Janet Hodgson would later reflect on the experience. She was bullied at school and nicknamed "Ghost Girl" due to the publicity.

"I knew when the voices were happening, of course. It felt like something was behind me all the time. They did all sorts of tests—filling my mouth with water and so on—but the voices still came out. The levitation was scary, because you didn't know where you were going to land. I remember a curtain being wound around my neck. I was screaming. I thought I was going to die."

Speaking in 2007, then in her early 40s, Janet remained convinced that the haunting was genuine:

"I know from my own experience that it was real... It lived off me, off my energy. Call me mad or a prankster if you like. Those events did happen. The poltergeist was with me—and I feel in a sense that he always will be."

The Enfield poltergeist case remains one of the most compelling and controversial incidents in the annals of psychic investigation. With over 30 eyewitnesses—including journalists, neighbours, and seasoned researchers—reporting phenomena ranging from object levitations and disembodied voices to full-body apparitions, the case defies easy explanation. It combined physical manifestations with psychological and emotional disturbances in a way rarely seen before or since. The level of documentation, including audio recordings, photographs, and written records from respected members of the Society for Psychical Research, elevates its importance.

The case's endurance also makes it stand out. It brought together key figures in the paranormal field, such as Maurice Grosse and Guy Lyon Playfair, whose differing investigative approaches enriched the documentation and analysis. Furthermore, the testimony of Janet Hodgson and others who experienced these events first-hand continues to resonate, not just as eerie recollections but as deeply personal accounts of an unexplained intrusion into domestic life.

Whether viewed as a powerful psychokinetic event sparked by psychological tension, or as a genuine haunting involving discarnate entities, the Enfield case has become a touchstone for both believers and sceptics. It invites ongoing debate about the nature of poltergeist activity, the role of adolescence and trauma, and the limits and potential bias of scientific inquiry into the paranormal.

In the end, the Enfield poltergeist was more than just a haunting. It was a challenge: to science, to belief, and to our understanding of reality itself. For that reason, it remains a cornerstone of psychical research—a case that still haunts the field, and refuses to be dismissed.

Chapter Nineteen

The Search for the Truth

Guy Lyon Playfair went on to write a book about the Enfield haunting, *This House is Haunted*. He had become interested in the paranormal during his time in Brazil, where he witnessed spiritual healing. Impressed by what he saw—he himself was treated for a stomach complaint using this technique—he continued investigating the subject.

One case that stood out involved a poltergeist in São Paulo in 1973, where a family reported loud bangs, crashes, and even clothes catching fire. Initially sceptical, Playfair was inclined to dismiss such phenomena as trickery. However, his perspective shifted after investigating this and other cases in Brazil.

One particularly strange case concerned Marcia, a 28-year-old woman who found a plaster statue on the beach. Her aunt told her it was a painted statue of the sea goddess Yemanjá and warned her to leave it, as it was likely left as an offering in return for a favor. Marcia ignored the warning and took it home.

Within days, she began experiencing a string of bad luck. A pressure cooker exploded, causing second-degree burns. The local Umbanda Centre—an Afro-Brazilian spiritual group—told her that the statue had brought a curse and must be returned to the beach. Marcia then noticed that the remaining paint patches on the statue matched her injuries. Even more disturbing were the paint patches on the statue's eyes. Terrified, she returned it to the seashore, after which her misfortunes abruptly ended.

Back in England, Playfair joined the Society for Psychical Research (SPR) and later gained fame through his investigation of the Enfield poltergeist. Over time, he came to believe that explaining poltergeists merely as psychic energy from troubled minds was insufficient. He suggested that these entities were mischievous, disembodied spirits. He once told author Colin Wilson that disturbed teenagers release a kind of "football" of energy during puberty. This ball of energy, according to Playfair, attracts two or three spirit entities who begin to "kick it around." When they get bored, they leave with the ball of energy, often leaving puddles of water behind—a detail noted in many poltergeist cases.

Wilson found Playfair's spirit-entity theory more compelling than most but also explored other ideas. In his book *Poltergeist!*, Wilson writes about *elementals*— beings associated with the four elements: air, water, fire, and earth. He speculated that poltergeists might be such elemental spirits, or *thought forms* generated by intense emotion.

Other occult writers, such as Elliott O'Donnell, believed that evil thoughts and actions could generate these entities. John Keel, in *Operation Trojan Horse*, also discussed elementals, noting that similar ideas appear in global folklore, from Ireland to Tibet.

In his book *Mysteries*, Colin Wilson describes how Alexandra David-Neel created a phantom monk, or *tulpa*, that appeared so solid it was even mistaken for a real person by a herdsman. However, she began to lose control of her creation, with the monk becoming increasingly hostile and malignant. It took her six months of concentrated effort to *dematerialise* it.

Colin Wilson.
Photo: Colin Wilson Estate.

Wilson also mentions the book *Psychic Self-Defence*, in which the author, Dion Fortune, writes about having negative thoughts toward someone who had wronged her. In a half-dozing state, she imagined the Nordic wolf god Fenrir and wondered how satisfying it would be to unleash him on her enemy. Suddenly, she felt a curious drawing-out sensation from her solar plexus, and there beside her on the bed appeared a large grey wolf, its back pressed against her. The creature looked at her and snarled, baring its teeth.

Terrified, but keeping her composure, she ordered it to leave the room. However, it soon began to terrorise the household. One female family member complained of dreams involving wolves. Upon waking, she saw the glowing eyes of a wild animal staring at her from the dark corner of her room.

Seeking advice from someone regarded as an expert and teacher in such matters, Fortune was told to abandon her desire for revenge, as it was feeding the creature's power. Summoning the entity once more, she reabsorbed it—eventually transforming it into a shapeless grey mist.

Some might dismiss these stories as fantasy. However, in 1972, the Toronto Society for Psychical Research, led by Dr. George Owen, ran a controlled experiment to test whether ghosts might be thought forms. The team invented a character named Philip Aylesford, who had lived in Diddington, Warwickshire, during the English Civil War. He had fallen in love with a gypsy girl, but his wife—upon discovering their affair—had the girl accused of witchcraft. She was burned at the stake. Heartbroken, Philip took his own life.

The group tried for several months to contact 'Philip' without success. Determined to strengthen the connection, one member even visited the location of Philip's fictional home in Diddington, Warwickshire, to take photographs of the church and surrounding old buildings. These images were intended to create a stronger mental link and lend credibility to their séances.

After some time, the group decided to adopt a more light-hearted and relaxed approach to their sessions. This change was inspired by reading papers from noted psychic researchers C. Brookes-Smith, D.W. Hunt, and K. J. Batcheldor. These researchers had studied 19th-century séances and concluded that a calm, informal atmosphere tended to produce better results, as opposed to the stiff and serious tone often associated with traditional spiritualism.

One evening, while the group was relaxing and singing songs together, the table they had been using suddenly began to vibrate noticeably. This unexpected activity encouraged them to hold further sessions. Gradually, 'Philip' made his presence known through rapping sounds on the table, answering questions about his life, and confirming details from his invented backstory. The phenomena escalated until the table was levitating and moving around the room on its own. On one memorable occasion, the table even tried to exit the room but became wedged in the doorway, much to the group's surprise.

Intriguingly, the group began to test Philip's 'knowledge' by asking about events and details not included in his fabricated story. Although Philip gave clear and confident responses, it was noted that these were not always historically accurate, suggesting either limitations in the phenomenon or the subconscious creation of information by the group members.

To better understand the nature of the sounds, the group decided to record the raps and knocks for acoustic analysis. Dr. Alan Gauld, a respected member of the Society for Psychical Research in England, examined the recordings and found that the knocks produced during the séances had a unique acoustic signature. Unlike typical human-made knocks, which start loudly and then fade gradually, Philip's knocks began loudly but dropped off into silence almost immediately. This pattern was consistent with analyses of raps recorded during alleged poltergeist events. In contrast, human knocks typically show a more prolonged decay in sound, confirming that the séance sounds were acoustically distinct and unlikely to have been produced by the participants themselves.

During the summer of 1974, the group decided to take a brief break from its weekly meetings. During this break, several team members reported experiencing poltergeist phenomena in their homes. Later, one member joked that if Philip did not answer them, they might send him away. Suddenly, the phenomenon stopped, and the group had to work hard to bring Philip back at the next session.

Another group in Toronto decided to try the experiment too, creating a character named *Lilith*. She was supposed to be a French Canadian in the French Resistance during World War II who got caught and executed by the Germans as a spy. After a few weeks, they started hearing raps and noticed the table moving, with *Lilith* even answering questions about her made-up life. Then, another group in Australia gave it a shot, inventing a teenage girl named *Skippy Cartman* who had been killed by her older boyfriend after she got pregnant. Eventually, they heard raps and scratching sounds and saw the table moving on its own.

So, did their experiments prove that poltergeists are only a product of the mind, as many researchers believe? The answer is no. Their attempts to replicate many aspects of poltergeist phenomena, such as the sudden appearance or disappearance of objects, met with failure. It is also worth noting that other groups attempting to replicate the phenomenon with similar techniques yielded no results. Colin Wilson remained unconvinced, pointing out that Philip's appearance came only after the group performed a series of traditional séances. Had Philip, he wondered, been just another bored spirit that joined the group for lack of anything better to do? After all, a poltergeist is happy to take on the identity its human observers believe it to be—a demon, the Devil, a witch, or even a cavalier named Philip.

Poltergeists have been with us throughout all recorded history. Yet, even in the 21st century, we are no closer to truly understanding them.

Poltergeists can cause fires, move furniture, make objects vanish and reappear, communicate through raps, and even take possession of someone. They can also be playful, indulge in pranks, tell lies, display violence, and take enormous pleasure in terrifying the households they choose to haunt. The phenomenon can last days, weeks, or, in some cases, years. Clearly, poltergeists follow certain behavioral patterns, even if these vary from case to case.

The fact that poltergeists use some form of energy to manifest themselves is evident. It is also clear that one or more individuals are the source of some or all of this energy. Guy Lyon Playfair suggested that someone entering puberty needs a channel or outlet for their newfound energy—sports or sexual activity could serve this purpose. However, if such an outlet is unavailable, the energy may leak into the external environment, allowing the poltergeist to use it. The same argument could also apply to older individuals experiencing mental anxiety or sexual stress.

Other theories suggest that poltergeists may draw on earth energies, such as ley lines or magnetic fields—especially those associated with water or rock formations. Playfair even suggested that poltergeists may exist in another dimension, where the laws of physics operate differently. This would explain why they are capable of scientifically impossible feats: making objects appear or disappear, reducing solid matter to powder, and transporting items through walls without leaving a trace.

This theory echoes the ideas of other researchers who believe that poltergeists might be intelligent, non-human energies that have accidentally entered our dimension and lash out in panic as they try to return to their own reality.

So what are poltergeists? Are they spirits of the dead? Thought forms? Psychic energy from the unconscious mind? Or something else entirely?

And do their displays of violence suggest something more sinister? When our ancestors blamed poltergeists for demonic possession, were they closer to the truth than we give them credit for? Are poltergeists some form of malignant entity that uses the energy of a disturbed human being, masquerading as friendly or playful until their true nature is revealed?

Perhaps "poltergeist" is a catch-all term, describing several distinct phenomena with different origins—spirits, elementals, thought forms, or something not yet understood by science.

Colin Wilson observed that poltergeists often throw temper tantrums until they are noticed, upon which they delight in the attention before moving on or fading away. Is this the key to ultimately understanding the poltergeist phenomenon?

Wilson, in his book on poltergeists, notes that what we term 'I'—our personality— is multilayered. He then quotes from Lyall Watson's book *The Romero Error*, in which Watson suggests that human beings may have a whole series of selves that, upon death, shed the physical body like a garment. The idea of multiple selves or levels is not unique to Watson's work; Madame Blavatsky and W. T. Stead have discussed it in their books. This belief is also found in Egyptian and Hindu occultism.

Wilson also notes how we can suddenly become immature, howling with anger if something does not go our way. We have all met, as he observes, well-balanced and strong-willed people who can instantly change when suddenly frustrated by something. It is as if a lower intelligence has taken over.

W. T. Stead's book *Real Ghost Stories* quotes an unnamed doctor who believed in the reality of multiple consciousnesses: "With regard to dual multiple consciousnesses, my own feeling has always been that the individuals stand behind the other in the chambers of the mind, or else, as it were, in concentric circles." Stead then compares this to the Jewish tabernacle, where a high priest watches over and guides the lesser egos that make up the human personality.

Stead, in the same book, refers to hypnotists who have brought forth multiple personalities from their patients when hypnotised. "It is evident," he wrote, "if the hypnotists are right, that the human body is more like a tenement house than a single [dwelling], and that the inmates love each other no more than the ordinary occupants of tenement property."

So are we more than one person sharing a single body? And do we possess a higher self, the superconscious, a guardian angel who controls our future based on a middle self—the conscious ego—that part of us that acts out our hopes and desires?

And is the poltergeist the lower self or soul, the part containing our baser impulses and desires, that bit of us closest to the animal world? After death, does this lower self separate from the middle and higher selves? And does it still retain some memory, rudimentary powers of reason, and the ability to draw energy from, among other things, a troubled, unsuspecting host or hosts?

We may never solve the mystery of the poltergeist. However, Colin Wilson may have come closer than anyone else to providing a solution. Are poltergeists lost and lonely fragmented souls, wandering from one person to another before finally fading into oblivion? If so, they deserve our pity rather than our fear.

Perhaps the real value of poltergeist phenomena lies not just in understanding the entities themselves—but in uncovering more about who we are.

Afterword

Alan Murdie on the Poltergeist Phenomenon

Looking back on this book, the clearest fact which emerges from John West's review of poltergeist cases through history is their persistence and the striking similarity between accounts of phenomena across so many years and different cultures. Had he wished, this book could have been far longer and still not exhausted the source material, and that is only sources published in English. Beyond this, also, an enormous foreign literature of poltergeists in other languages awaits exploration.

What is also apparent is no one explanation can account for all credible poltergeist cases since no one explanation fits all the facts.

The challenge remains: can some sense be made from such an ocean of data? Are we no further advanced than Harry Price at Borley Rectory in the 1930s and 1940s?

Over the years I knew him, I shared many conversations with the late Guy Playfair on the subject of paranormal phenomena, poltergeists in particular.

A few months before he died in April 2018, he said, "I've been studying poltergeists for 45 years, and I am still just as puzzled as to what causes them as at the beginning."

In pursuit of possible explanations, Guy had recently begun corresponding with Dr Jaques Vallee, the world's most knowledgeable ufologist, who had remarked briefly on poltergeist phenomena in a book many years earlier. Here a distinction can be made; whereas over the years the appearance of alleged phenomena (and the alleged aliens) has changed, suggesting that the roots may lie in changing social beliefs and human fashions, in contrast the poltergeist has spanned the centuries, the character of its standard tricks and behaviour remaining remarkably consistent. All commentators agree this baffling physicality is a primary feature of the poltergeist; the poltergeist snatches the limelight, and its effects being physical are harder to deny (they are clearly not in someone's head when a table turns over or a glass explodes). It is also quite obvious in terms of force and variety that the effects reported far exceed results from psychokinesis experiments, 'mind over matter', achieved in parapsychology laboratories across the world since the 1930s.

Trying to bring forward some order into the plethora and chaos of details, Dr Alan Gauld, in his book *Poltergeists* (1979), studied 500 historic poltergeist cases. Undertaking a computer analysis of this substantial sample, he found

76% of poltergeist cases lasting six months or less with disturbances centring on particular individuals. This was suggestive of a purely mental origin or link with a living individual or human agency,, with more females than males as the postulated foci. However, as mentioned, 24% of longer-term cases (1 year or more) seemed unconnected with an individual and appeared to be more place-centred, involving small object movements, footsteps and doors opening by themselves.

One hears these stories quite a lot in old British pubs (a reason to doubt them, you might think). But they arise not just in pubs — other buildings generate reports; if anyone collects them, they will soon find they are too widespread or persistent to be the result of hoaxes.

Gauld found such longer-term poltergeists display noticeable differences with the shorter cases in being closer to the traditional idea of a haunting and suggesting influence from an external haunting presence, perhaps engaging in a rudimentary form of communication at times. Gauld's cluster analysis confirmed the suspicions of earlier researchers, such as physicist Sir William Barrett's observation in a 1911 volume of the *Proceedings* of the Society for Psychical Research (vol. 25 pp. 317-412) that 'the disturbances may be centred on persons of either sex and appear to be attached to a particular place as well as to a particular person'. At the beginning of his career, in 1877 at Derrygonnelly in Ireland, Barrett encountered a poltergeist in a rural cottage which made raps. Engaging in rudimentary communication by way of knocks, Barrett found the poltergeist could know the number he was thinking of, suggesting some kind of telepathy was operating – the question is with who or what?

The patterns found by Gauld started to make sense of what otherwise would have remained a superficially amorphous collection of facts and isolated accounts. Some of the similarities in the types of phenomena (for example, the strange acoustic properties detected in instrumental analysis) are so striking that they would count as evidence in a judicial context. Known as 'similar fact evidence', where striking similarities arise, they may become proof of causation or guilt in cases of serial offending, capable of proving a disputed fact beyond reasonable doubt.

The fact that there are patterns in the data indicates that some sort of real effect is operating, indicating some rules govern the poltergeist, including ones where signs of an external intelligence are shown. This is a difficulty for materialist models of the mind that believe that consciousness must rest in the brain and ceases on death.

Another troubling area is those cases where the individual is harmed or subject to unwelcome and sometimes brutal force. It was this factor reported at Pontefract in 1968 that made Colin Wilson change his mind over the unconscious mind being at work, convincing himself it was a spirit interference when he came to it over ten years later. However, I would hesitate to embrace the unquiet spirit explanation as the immediate alternative for this or presume that 19th-century spiritualists were necessarily right (modern psychology and psychiatry have come to realise how some people readily self-harm, for instance).

Indeed, whilst undoubtedly similarities can be discerned between widely separated cases, closer examination shows that there can also be a wide variation of phenomena; many odd elements and peculiarities also appear which appear to refute easy explanation and models hitherto examined. Philosopher and psychologist William James (1842-1910) referred to how "the accredited and orderly facts of every science there ever floats a sort of dust-cloud of exceptional observations, of occurrences minute and irregular and seldom met with," that are often dismissed or ignored by mainstream science; poltergeists provide a prime example.

Sceptical theories – often by armchair critics years after the event with little or no insights into original data – propose explanations without a shred of evidence to back them up. One can see why Maurice Grosse eschewed theories at Enfield in 1977-79 around causation, though he was personally of the belief the effects could not arise from the minds of the girls or the Hodgson family alone.

This difficulty with establishing a theory which can fit the facts makes it clear to me we must change our focus in studies of the poltergeist.

So, what is to be done? I have three suggestions. The first is to reanalyse these cases that John West reviews here wherever documentation, primary and secondary, will survive, and there may be many new facts and perspectives to uncover with cases examined in light of 21st-century perspectives and advances.

In this John's collection here provides already a sampler of some of the most striking cases where evidence in one form or another may survive and be accessible.

Secondly, it is to devote some thinking to the physical aspects. Tying up these reports and experiences with what is already known or speculated upon in conventional science, extending our boundaries of our knowledge strikes me as the key task.

It should not be forgotten that the poltergeist is defined by actual objective effects which appear to surpass the accepted laws of nature or, at least, subject them to some revision. Examples include the incendiary effects and the claim that objects moved or which appear as apports are warm to the touch.

Given that such objects often appear to materialise out of thin air or, in the case of stones being thrown, their source of origin cannot be identified, would a heating effect be expected on the surface in the case of an object moved through a hypothetical fourth or higher dimension?

Would they be found to contain traces of atmospheric gases within their material substance if they had apparently materialised out of the air ? Also, do identifiable physical traces of some kind endure on some level within objects which are moved or rearranged which may be detectable? Anomalous electrical effects are often reported in 'haunted' houses with lights flickering or inexplicable breakdowns in electrical gadgets and equipment – what kind of electromagnetic or other force or energy could accomplish this? These are the sorts of questions that need to be addressed.

Thirdly, fresh thinking must be given to the social aspects, especially from the position of the troubled households at the centre of these baffling disturbances.

Why this family? What has gone on in their lives and history? What is there that has particularised them to find themselves in a ghost-shattered home? What are their personal and familial medical histories and circumstances and their overall state of health, individual and collective; are there certain organic or psychological conditions and symptoms that predominate as a backdrop for poltergeist outbreaks? Though hard to discover, such facts are theoretically obtainable, and since the millennium, 'clinical parapsychology' has started to develop as a subset of academic paranormal research. Poltergeist cases hold out the prospect of providing actual data for such research.

And what of the wider social aspects to be considered, given families do not live in a vacuum? Within medicine as a whole, it has been belatedly recognised that issues such as fertility, health and illness may be best understood, not just as objectively measurable states, but as socially influenced categories and labels negotiated by professionals, sufferers and others within the wider social-cultural context in which troubled individuals are thrust.

Perhaps we need to revisit our ideas of adolescence and psychological development. Is the connection as close as has often` been thought? These are questions and challenges that can engage us with poltergeist research as the 21st century advance.

Appendix

The Epworth Rectory Haunting

The Wesleys—Men of Rank, Reason, and Reverence

The accounts of the strange disturbances at Epworth Rectory in 1716–1717 are rendered all the more compelling by the stature and character of the men who recorded them: Samuel Wesley, the Anglican rector of Epworth, and his son John Wesley, who would go on to found the Methodist movement. These were not fanciful men given to idle superstition. On the contrary, both were learned scholars, clergymen of high moral standing, and deeply devout Christians who lived according to the principles of reason and faith.

Samuel Wesley, educated at Oxford and a prolific theological writer, was a man of the cloth in an age when clerical integrity was often a public benchmark of virtue. His adherence to discipline, prayer, and intellectual inquiry meant that he approached claims of the supernatural not with credulity but with cautious scrutiny. Similarly, John Wesley, later one of the most influential religious figures of the 18th century, was a man of rigorous logic and discipline. His trust in divine providence was accompanied by a rational, orderly approach to experience—spiritual or otherwise.

What lends further weight to their testimonies is that both men accepted the possibility of supernatural activity not as an affront to reason but as consistent with their Christian worldview. In an age where belief in the invisible world—of angels, demons, and divine intervention—was seen not as irrational but as part of the fabric of reality, their reports were not dismissed by contemporaries but taken seriously by clergy and laity alike.

That John Wesley, later a pioneer of Enlightenment-era revivalist preaching, took the time to record the experiences of his family with forensic care speaks volumes. Likewise, Samuel Wesley's detailed journal entries—frank, methodical, and devoid of sensationalism—demonstrate a man more interested in truth than notoriety.

Their conviction that these disturbances could not be reduced to trickery or natural causes reveals a world in which the boundary between the physical and spiritual realms was not only thin but active.

In this context, *The Epworth Rectory Haunting* is not merely a ghost story. It is a window into the devout minds of two eminent religious men. Their social rank, intellectual credibility, and spiritual seriousness compel us to consider their accounts not with scepticism alone, but with the thoughtful attention they intended.

I. Account by John Wesley
From The Arminian Magazine, No. 7, 1784
An Account of the Disturbances in My Father's House

When I was very young, I heard several letters read, wrote to my elder brother by my father, giving an account of strange disturbances, which were in his house, at Epworth, in Lincolnshire. When I went down thither, in the year 1720, I carefully enquired into the particulars. I spoke to each of the persons who were then in the house, and took down what each could testify of his or her own knowledge. The sum of which was this.

1. On December 2, 1716, while Robert Brown, my father's servant, was sitting with one of the maids a little before ten at night, in the dining-room which opened into the garden, they both heard one knocking at the door. Robert rose and opened it, but could see nobody. Quickly it knocked again and groaned. "It is Mr. Turpin," said Robert, "he had the stone and used to groan so." He opened the door again twice or thrice, the knocking being twice or thrice repeated. But still seeing nothing, and being a little startled, they rose and went up to bed.

2. When Robert came to the top of the garret stairs, he saw a hand-mill, which was at a little distance, whirled about very swiftly. When he related this he said,

"Nought vexed me, but that it was empty. I thought, if it had but been full of malt he might have ground his heart out for me."

When he was in bed, he heard as it were the gobbling of a turkey-cock, close to the bedside, and soon after, the sound of one stumbling over his shoes and boots. But there were none there; he had left them below.

3. The next day, he and the maid related these things to the other maid, who laughed heartily, and said,

"What a couple of fools are you? I defy anything to fright me."

After churning in the evening, she put the butter in the tray, and had no sooner carried it into the dairy, than she heard a knocking on the shelf where pancheons of milk stood, first above the shelf, then below. She took the candle and searched both above and below; but being able to find nothing, threw down butter, tray and all, and ran away for life.

4. The next evening between five and six o'clock my sister Molly, then about twenty years of age, sitting in the dining-room, reading, heard as if it were the door that led into the hall open, and a person walking in, that seemed to have on a silk nightgown, rustling and trailing along. It seemed to walk round her, then to the door, then round again; but she could see nothing,

She thought, "It signifies nothing to run away, for whatever it is, it can run faster than me." So she rose, put her book under her arm, and walked slowly away.

5. After supper, she was sitting with my sister Suky (about a year older than her) in one of the chambers, and telling her what had happened, she quite made light of it, telling her,

"I wonder you are so easily frighted: I would fain see what would fright me." Presently a knocking began under the table. She took the candle and looked, but could find nothing. Then the iron casement began to clatter, and the lid of a warmingpan. Next the latch of the door moved up and down without ceasing. She started up, leaped into the bed without undressing, pulled the bedclothes over her head, and never ventured to look up till next morning.

6. A night or two after, my sister Hetty, a year younger than my sister Molly, was waiting as usual, between nine and ten to take away my father's candle, when she heard one coming down the garret stairs, walking slowly by her; then going down the best stairs, then up the back stairs, and up the garret stairs. And at every step, it seemed the house shook from top to bottom. Just then my father knocked. She went in, took his candle, and got to bed as fast as possible.

7. In the morning she told this to my eldest sister, who told her,

"You know, I believe none of these things. Pray let me take away the candle tonight, and I will find out the trick." She accordingly took away the candle, then she heard a noise below. She hastened down stairs, to the hall, where the noise was.

But it was then in the kitchen. She ran into the kitchen where it was drumming on the inside of the screen. When she went round it was drumming on the outside, and so always on the opposite side to her. Then she heard a knocking at the back-kitchen door. She ran to it, unlocked it softly, and when the knocking was repeated, suddenly opened it: but nothing was to be seen. As soon as she had shut it, the knocking began again: she opened it again, but could see nothing: when she went to shut the door, it was violently thrust against her: she let it fly open; but nothing appeared. She went again to shut it, and it was again thrust against her: but she set her knee and her shoulder to the door: forced it to, and turned the key. Then the knocking began again: but she let it go on, and went up to bed. However from that time she was thoroughly convinced, that there was no imposter in the affair.

8. The next morning my sister telling my mother what had happened, she said, "If I hear anything myself, I shall know how to judge."

Soon after, she [Emily] begged her [mother] to come into the nursery. She did, and heard in the corner of the room, as it were the violent rocking of a cradle; but no cradle had been there for some years. She was convinced it was preternatural, and earnestly prayed it might not disturb her in her own chamber at the hours of retirement. And it never did.

She now thought it was proper to tell my father. But he was extremely angry, and said,

"Suky, I am ashamed of you. These boys and girls fright one another; but you are a woman of sense, and should know better. Let me hear of it no more."

At six in the evening, he had family prayers as usual. When he began the prayer for the king, a knocking began all round the room, and a thundering knock attended the Amen. The same was heard from this time every morning and evening while the prayer for the king was repeated.

As both my father and mother are now at rest, and incapable of being pained thereby, I think it my duty to furnish the serious reader with a key to this circumstance. The year before King William died, my father observed my mother did not say "Amen" to the Prayer for the king. She said she could not, for she did not believe the Prince of Orange was king. He vowed he would never cohabit with her till she did. He then took his horse and rode away, nor did she hear anything of him for a twelvemonth. He then came back and lived with her as before. But I fear his vow was not forgotten before God.

9. Being informed that Mr. Hoole, the Vicar of Haxey (an eminently pious and sensible man) could give me some further information, I walked over to him. He said,

"Robert Brown came over to me, and told me, your father desired my company. When I came he gave me an account of all that had happened, particularly the knocking during family prayer. But that evening (to my great satisfaction) we had no knocking at all. But between nine and ten, a servant came in and said, Old Jeffries is coming (that was the name of one that died in the house) for I hear the signal. This they informed me was heard every night about a quarter before ten. It was toward the top of the house on the outside, at the northeast corner, resembling a loud creaking of a saw, or rather that of a windmill when the body of it is turned about in order to shift the sails to the wind. We then heard a knocking over our heads, and Mr. Wesley catching up a candle, said,

'Come, Sir, now you shall hear for yourself.'

We went upstairs; he with much hope and I (to say the truth) with much fear. When we came into the nursery, it was knocking in the next room: when we were there, it was knocking in the nursery. And there it continued to knock, though we came in, particularly at the head of the bed, (which was of wood) in which Miss Hetty and two of her younger sisters lay. Mr. Wesley observing that they were much affected though asleep, sweating and trembling exceedingly; was very angry, and pulling out a pistol, was going to fire at the place from whence the sound came. But I catched him by the arm and said,

'Sir, you are convinced this is something preternatural. If so, you cannot hurt it, but you give it power to hurt you.' He then went to the place and said sternly,

'Thou deaf and dumb devil, why dost thou fright these children that cannot answer for themselves? Come to me in my study, that am a man?' Instantly it knocked his knock (the particular knock which he always used at the gate) as if it would shiver the board in pieces, and we heard nothing more that night."

10. Till this time, my father had never heard the least disturbance in his study. But the next evening, as he attempted to go into his study (of which none had any key but himself) when he opened the door, it was thrust back with such violence as had like to have thrown him down. However, he thrust the door open and went in. Presently there was knocking first on one side, then on the other; and after a time, in the next room, wherein my sister Nancy was. He went into that room and (the noise continuing) adjured it to speak, but in vain. He then said,

"These spirits love darkness; put out the candle and perhaps it will speak." She did so, and he repeated his adjuration, but still there was only knocking and no articulate sound. Upon this he said,

"Nancy, two Christians are an over-match for the devil. Go all of you downstairs; it may be, when I am alone, he will have courage to speak." When she was gone, a thought came in and he said,

"If thou art the spirit of my son Samuel, I pray, knock three knocks and no more." Immediately all was silence, and there was no more knocking at all that night.

11. I asked my sister Nancy (then about fifteen years old) whether she was not afraid, when my father used that adjuration? She answered, She was sadly afraid it would speak, when she put out the candle: but she was not at all afraid in the day time, when it walked after her, as she swept the chambers, as it constantly did, and seemed to sweep after her. Only she thought he might have done it for her, and saved her the trouble.

12. By the time all my sisters were so accustomed to these noises, that they gave them little disturbance. A gentle tapping at their bed-head usually began between nine and ten at night. They then commonly said to each other,

"Jeffrey is coming: it is time to go to sleep." And if they heard a noise in the day, and said to my youngest sister,

"Hark, Kezzy, Jeffrey is knocking above, she would run up stairs, and pursue it from room to room, saying she desired no better diversion.

13. A few nights after, my father and mother were just gone to bed and the candle was not taken away, when they heard three blows, and a second, and a third three, as it were with a large oaken staff struck upon a chest which stood by the bedside. My father immediately arose, put on his nightgown, and hearing great noises below, took the candle and went down. My mother walked by his side. As they went down the broad stairs, they heard as if a vessel full of silver was poured upon my mother's breast and ran jingling down to her feet. Quickly after there was a sound as if a large iron ball was thrown among many bottles under the stairs. But nothing was hurt. Soon after our large mastiff dog came and ran to shelter himself between them. While the disturbances continued, he used to bark and leap, and snap on one side and the other, and that frequently, before any person in the room heard any noise at all. But after two or three days, he used to tremble and creep away before the noise began. And by this, the family knew it was at hand; nor did the observation ever fail.

A little before my father and mother came into the hall, it seemed as if a very large coal was violently thrown upon the floor and dashed all in pieces. But nothing was seen. My father then cried out,

"Suky, do you not hear? All the pewter is thrown about in the kitchen."

But when they looked, all the pewter stood in its place. There then was a loud knocking at the back door. My father opened it, but saw nothing. It was then at the fore door. He opened that; but it was still soft labour. After opening first the one, then the other several times, he turned and went up to bed. But the noises were so violent all over the house, that he could not sleep till four in the morning.

14. Several gentlemen and clergymen now earnestly advised my father to quit the house. But he constantly answered, "No; let the devil flee from me; I will never flee from the devil." But he wrote to my eldest brother at London, to come down. He was preparing so to do, when another letter came, informing him the disturbances were over, after they had continued (the latter part of the time, day and night) from the second of December to the end of January.

John Wesley
Hilton Park
March 26, 1784

I. Journal of Rev. Samuel Wesley

An Account of Noises and Disturbances in my House, at Epworth, Lincolnshire, in December and January, 1716.

From the first of December, my children and servants heard many strange noises, groans, knockings, etc. in every story, and most of the rooms of my house. But I heard nothing of it myself, they would not tell me for some time, because, according to the vulgar opinion, if it boded any ill to me, I could not hear it. When it increased, and the family could not easily conceal it, they told me of it.

My daughters Susanna and Ann, were below stairs in the dining room, and heard first at the doors, then over their heads, and the night after a knocking under their feet, though nobody was in the chambers or below them. The like they and my servants heard in both the kitchens, at the door against the partition, and over them.

The maid servant heard groans as of a dying man. My daughter Emilia coming down stairs to draw up the clock, and lock the doors at ten at night, as usual, heard under the staircase a sound among some bottles there, as if they had been all dashed to pieces; but when she looked, all was safe.

Something, like the steps of a man, was heard going up and down stairs, at all hours of the night, and vast rumblings below stairs, and in the garrets. My man, who lay in the garret, heard someone come slaring through the garret to his chamber, rattling by his side, as if against his shoes, though he had none there; at other times walking up and down stairs, when all the house were in bed, and gobbling like a turkey cock. Noises were heard in the nursery, and all the other chambers; knocking first at the feet of the bed and behind it; and a sound like that of dancing in a matted chamber, next the nursery, when the door was locked and nobody in it.

My wife would have persuaded them it was rats within doors, and some unlucky people knocking without; till at last we heard several loud knocks in our own chamber, on my side of the bed; but till, I think, the 21st at night I heard nothing of it. That night I was waked a little before one, by nine distinct very loud knocks, which seemed to be in the next room to ours, with a sort of a pause at every third stroke. I thought it might be somebody without the house, and having got a stout mastiff, hoped he would soon rid me of it.

The next night I heard six knocks, but not so loud as the former. I know not whether it was in the morning after Sunday the 23rd, when about seven my daughter Emily called her mother into the nursery, and told her she might now hear the noises there. She went in, and heard it at the bedsteads, then under the bed, then at the head of it. She knocked, and it answered her. She looked under the bed, and thought something ran from thence, but could not well tell of what shape, but thought it most like a badger.

The next night but one, we were awakened about one, by the noises, which were so violent it was in vain to think of sleep while they continued. I rose, and my wife would rise with me. We went into every chamber and down stairs; and generally as we went into one room, we heard it in that behind us, though all the family had been in bed several hours. When we were going down stairs, and at the bottom of them, we heard, as Emily had done before, a clashing among the bottles, as if they had been broke all to pieces, and another sound distinct from it, as if a peck of money had been thrown down before us. The same, three of my daughters heard at another time.

We went through the hall into the kitchen, when our mastiff came whining to us, as he did always after the first night of its coming; for then he barked violently at it, but was silent afterwards, and seemed more afraid than any of the children. We still heard it rattle and thunder in every room above or behind us, locked as well as open, except my study, where as yet it never came. After two, we went to bed, and were pretty quiet the rest of the night.

Wednesday night, December 26., after, or a little before ten, my daughter Emilia heard the signal of its beginning to play, with which she was perfectly acquainted; it was like the strong winding up of a jack. She called us, and I went into the nursery, where it used to be most violent. The rest of the children were asleep. It began with knocking in the kitchen underneath, then seemed to be at the bed's feet, then under the bed, at last at the head of it. I went down stairs, and knocked with my stick against the joists of the kitchen. It answered me as often and as loud as I knocked; but then I knocked as I usually do at my door, 1 – 2 3 4 5 6 – 7, but this puzzled it, and it did not answer, or not in the same method; though the children heard it do the same exactly twice or thrice after.

I went up stairs, and found it still knocking hard, though with some respite, sometimes under the bed, sometimes at the bed's head. I observed my children that they were frightened in their sleep, and trembled very much till it waked them. I stayed there alone, bid them go to sleep, and sat at the bed's feet by them, when the noise began again. I asked what it was, and why it disturbed innocent children, and did not come to me in my study, if it had any thing to say to me. Soon after it gave one knock on the outside of the house. All the rest were within, and knocked off for that night.

I went out of doors, sometimes alone, at others with company, and walked round the house, but could see or hear nothing. Several nights the latch of our lodging chamber would be lifted up very often, when all were in bed. One night, when the noise was great in the kitchen, and on a deal partition, and the door in the yard, the latch whereof was often lifted up, my daughter Emilia went and held it fast on the inside, but it was still lifted up, and the door pushed violently against her, though nothing was to be seen on the outside.

When we were at prayers, and came to the prayers for King George, and the Prince, it would make a great noise over our heads constantly, whence some of the family called it a Jacobite. I have been thrice pushed by an invisible power, once against the corner of my desk in the study, a second time against the door of the matted chamber, a third time against the right side of the frame of my study door, as I was going in.

I followed the noise into almost every room in the house, both by day and by night, with lights and without, and have sat alone for some time, and when I heard the noise, spoke to it to tell me what it was, but never heard any articulate voice, and only once or twice two or three feeble squeaks, a little louder than the chirping of a bird, but not like the noise of rats, which I have often heard.

I had designed on Friday, December the 28th, to make a visit to a friend, Mr. Downs, at Normandy, and stay some days with him, but the noises were so boisterous on Thursday night, that I did not care to leave my family. So I went to Mr.

Hoole, of Haxsey, and desired his company on Friday night. He came; and it began after ten, a little later than ordinary. The younger children were gone to bed, the rest of the family and Mr. Hoole were together in the matted chamber. I sent the servants down to fetch in some fuel, went with them, and staid in the kitchen till they came in. When they were gone, I heard loud noises against the doors and partition, and at length the usual signal, though somewhat after the time. I had never heard it before, but knew it by the description my daughter had given me. It was much like the turning about of a windmill when the wind changes. When the servants returned, I went up to the company, who had heard all the other noises below, but not the signal. We heard all the knocking as usual, from one chamber to another, but at its going off, like the rubbing of a beast against the wall; but from that time till January the 24th, we were quiet.

Having received a letter from Samuel the day before relating to it, I read what I had written of it to my family; and this day at morning prayer, the family heard the usual knocks at the prayer for the King. At night they were more distinct, both in the prayer for the King, and that for the Prince; and one very loud knock at the amen was heard by my wife, and most of my children, at the inside of my bed. I heard nothing myself. After nine, Robert Brown sitting alone by the fire in the back kitchen, something came out of the copper hole like a rabbit but less, and turned round five times very swiftly. Its ears lay flat upon its neck, and its little scut stood straight up. He ran after it with the tongs in his hands, but when he could find nothing, he was frightened, and went to the maid in the parlour.

On Friday, the 25th, having prayers at church, I shortened, as usual, those in the family at morning, omitting the confession, absolution, and prayers for the king and prince. I observed, when this is done, there is no knocking. I therefore used them one morning for a trial; at the name of King George, it began to knock, and did the same when I prayed for the Prince. Two knocks I heard, but took no notice after prayers, till after all who were in the room, ten persons besides me, spoke of it, and said they heard it. No noise at all the rest of the prayers.

Sunday, January 27. Two soft strokes at the morning prayers for King George, above stairs.

About John West

John West is a Suffolk-based film producer, actor, broadcaster, and author with a lifelong passion for history, the paranormal, and storytelling in all its forms. Born in Edmonton, North London, he has developed a rich and varied career across radio, television, publishing, and film.

John is the author of several well-regarded books on British history, ghosts, and folklore, including *Britain's Haunted Heritage* (2019), *Britain's Ghostly Heritage* and *The Battle of Gainsborough 1643* (2022), and *Britain's Haunted Land* (2023). His writing also features regularly in *Psychic News* and *Suffolk and Norfolk Life*, covering everything from celebrity interviews to investigations into legendary hauntings.

His passion for storytelling extends into broadcasting, with a long-standing background in radio. John has presented at six different radio stations—including BBC Radio Suffolk—and has hosted several hundred shows. He has played an active role in charity radio events, including co-organising and promoting an all-female charity bike ride and helping raise funds for SSAFA, the Armed Forces charity.

As a documentarian, John has written and contributed to several historical and paranormal-themed projects, including features on Jack the Ripper and poltergeists, blending in-depth research with compelling storytelling. One of his historical guides, *Roman Lincoln*, was adapted into a BBC Radio Lincolnshire documentary in which he also co-presented.

John's television appearances include work as the regular studio historian on Mustard TV, where he explored topics from Roman Britain to The Beatles. He's also been a guest on London Live TV, discussing the life and legacy of photographer Simon Marsden.

In the film world, John has worked on both sides of the camera. He appeared in productions such as *Detectorists* (BBC), *The Crown* (Netflix), *The Personal History of David Copperfield*, and *Boudica: Queen of War*. As a producer, he has collaborated with filmmaker Jason Figgis on numerous projects. Their credits include *The Ghost of Winifred Meeks*, *The Grey Man*, and four documentaries: *Maverick*, *Shirley Baker: Life Through a Lens* (which John wrote), *Colin Wilson: His Life and Work* (to which he contributed research and script material), and *Love?* He also wrote the narration for *Father of Dracula*, a documentary on

Bram Stoker currently in production. Another project, a documentary on Jack the Ripper (co-written with Michael Hawley), is also in production.

In 2022, John produced a series of celebration videos for the late Queen's Platinum Jubilee, directed and edited by Figgis.

Whether behind a microphone, a camera, or a keyboard, John West is dedicated to making history, folklore, and storytelling accessible, engaging, and meaningful to modern audiences.

John West.
Photo by Jason Figgis.

Recommended Reading

The Bell Witch: A Mysterious Spirit
Author: Charles Bailey Bell
Published: 1934
Publisher: Lark Bindery
Summary: Written by a descendant of the Bell family, this early account details America's most famous poltergeist case.

The Bell Witch: The Full Account
Author: Pat Fitzhugh
Published: 2000
Publisher: Armand Press
Summary: A detailed and critically sourced history of the Bell Witch case.

The Black Monk of Pontefract: The World's Most Violent and Relentless Poltergeist
Authors: Richard Estep and Bil Bungay
Published: 2019
Publisher: Independently published
Summary: Offers a comprehensive exploration of one of the most notorious poltergeist cases in British history.

The Cock Lane Ghost
Author: Paul Chambers
Published: 2006
Publisher: Sutton Publishing
Summary: A detailed and critically sourced history of the Cock Lane case.

The Encyclopedia of Ghosts and Spirits
Authors: John and Anne Spencer
Published: 1992
Publisher: Headline Book Publishing
Summary: Broad reference guide including poltergeist entries and historical cases.

Explaining the Unexplained: Mysteries of the Paranormal
Authors: Hans J. Eysenck & Carl Sargent
Published: 1982
Publisher: Weidenfeld & Nicolson
Summary: Scientific and sceptical perspectives on psychic and paranormal phenomena, including poltergeists.

Mysteries
Author: Colin Wilson
Originally Published: 1978
Reissued: 2020
Publisher: Watkins Publishing
Summary: While not exclusively about poltergeists, this volume addresses them in the broader context of psychic phenomena.

The Night Side of Nature
Author: Catherine Crowe
Published: 1848
Publisher: T.C. Newby
Summary: One of the earliest English-language collections discussing ghostly and poltergeist phenomena, blending folklore, anecdote, and early psychical theory.

Operation Trojan Horse
Author: John Keel
Published: 1970
Publisher: Putnam
Summary: A groundbreaking work that reinterprets UFO phenomena as part of a broader spectrum of paranormal activity.

Poltergeist!
Various Authors (Fortean Times)
Published: 2024
Publisher: Fortean Times
Summary: A collection of recent essays, case studies, and reprints on poltergeist phenomena from the Fortean Times archive.

Poltergeist!: A Study in Destructive Haunting
Author: Colin Wilson
Published: 1981
Publisher: New English Library
Summary: In-depth look at poltergeists worldwide; combines psychological, paranormal, and philosophical insights.

Poltergeist Over England
Author: Harry Price
Published: 1945
Publisher: Country Life Ltd.
Summary: A comprehensive survey of British poltergeist cases by one of the UK's first ghost hunters.

Poltergeist Over Scotland
Author: Geoff Holder
Published: 2013
Publisher: The History Press
Summary: Documents dozens of Scottish poltergeist cases from ancient history to modern times.

Poltergeists
Authors: Alan Gauld & A.D. Cornell
Originally Published: 1979
Reissue: 2018
Publisher: White Crow Books
Summary: Academic analysis of global poltergeist cases, still referenced today.

Poltergeists: A History of Violent Ghostly Phenomena
Author: P. G. Maxwell-Stuart
Published: 2011
Publisher: Amberley
Summary: A historical and cultural analysis of how poltergeists have been interpreted over time.

Poltergeists: Examining Mysteries of the Paranormal
Author: Michael Clarkson
Published: 2006
Publisher: Firefly Books
Summary: Investigative journalism approach to poltergeist activity, exploring psychological and environmental theories.

Psychic Self-Defence
Author: Dion Fortune
Published: 1930
Publisher: Rider & Co
Summary: A classic work on spiritual and psychic protection. Drawing on her own experiences, Fortune outlines various types of psychic attacks and offers practical techniques for recognizing, resisting, and guarding against occult influences and negative energies.

Real Ghost Stories
Author: W.T. Stead
Published: 1921
Publisher: Stead's Publishing House
Summary: Explores a range of phenomena, including apparitions, premonitions, and instances of dual personalities, offering insights into the Victorian fascination with the paranormal.

The Romeo Error: A Matter of Life and Death
Author: Lyall Watson
Published: 1974
Publisher: Doubleday
Summary: A thought-provoking exploration of the concept of death, challenging conventional perceptions and delving into the mysteries surrounding human consciousness and mortality.

This House Is Haunted: The True Story of the Enfield Poltergeist
Author: Guy Lyon Playfair
Originally Published: 1980
Reissued: 2011
Publisher: White Crow Books
Summary: The definitive account of the Enfield case.

Other books by John West

Roman Lincoln
Published: 1991. Second Edition: 1998
Publisher: Paul Watkins

Oliver Cromwell and the Battle of Gainsborough
Published: 1992
Publisher: Richard Kay

Studies in Scarlet
Published: 1994
Publisher: Casdec Ltd

Roman York
Published: 1995
Publisher: Richard Netherwood Ltd

Britain's Haunted Heritage
Published: 2019
Publisher: JMD Media

Britain's Ghostly Heritage
Published: 2022
Publisher: JMD Media

The Battle of Gainsborough 1643
Published: 2022
Publisher: JMD Media

Britain's Haunted Land
Published: 2023
Publisher: JMD Media

www.ingramcontent.com/pod-product-compliance
Lightning Source LLC
Chambersburg PA
CBHW070459100426
42743CB00010B/1680